LOYALTY

Sarah Helm

LOYALTY

OBERON BOOKS
LONDON

WWW.OBERONBOOKS.COM

First published in 2011 by Oberon Books Ltd
521 Caledonian Road, London N7 9RH
Tel: +44 (0) 20 7607 3637 / Fax: +44 (0) 20 7607 3629
e-mail: info@oberonbooks.com
www.oberonbooks.com

A catalogue record for this book is available from the British
Library.

PB ISBN: 978-1-84943-209-2
E ISBN: 978-1-84943-724-0

Cover design by SWD

Visit www.oberonbooks.com to read more about all our books
and to buy them. You will also find features, author interviews and
news of any author events, and you can sign up for e-newsletters
so that you're always first to hear about our new releases.

FOREWORD

LOYALTY

Essay by
Sherard Cowper-Coles

What do you do when the man you love, the father of your children, is deeply involved professionally in a project which you believe with every fibre of your being to be profoundly wrong? How do you cope when his work, and his boss, come crashing all the time into the home life of your young family?

Sarah Helm's remarkable play works at so many levels. In part, it is a moving account of how a relationship based on deep mutual understanding and respect somehow coped with the most impossible strains.

But in a larger sense it documents real events of great historical importance. Of course, it is a play, it is fiction. Yet it is also a *roman à clef*, in which we all know that Laura is really Sarah Helm, Nick is her partner Jonathan Powell (Tony Blair's Chief of Staff), Tony is Tony, Alastair is Alastair (Campbell), and Jack is Jack (Straw), and so on.

So in one, and perhaps the most important sense, it is an up-close, insider's, account of what it felt like to be living with the daily agonies of deciding to invade Iraq, and then finding out that the original justification for the war – that Saddam Hussein had Weapons of Mass Destruction – did not exist, and had been based on false intelligence.

As with Robert Harris's devastating *Ghost*, about a fictional ghost writer for Tony Blair's memoirs, or Joe Klein's *Primary Colors*, about the Bill Clinton Presidential Campaign, so with Sarah's *Loyalty*. Even if the plot is not literally true, the characterisation is authentic – alarmingly so.

Sarah Helm has a reporter's eye, and a true writer's ear for language, that paint an utterly convincing picture of living with Tony Blair's chief aide through turbulent times. She captures the cadences of Blair's speech, the way in which the No. 10 switchboard operates, all the details of what happens when one's home becomes an antechamber of government.

But her play is much more than that. It is also a journey to what is now another country, the world in the weeks and months after 9/11. We forget now the fear we all felt, and the way in which George Bush and others used what Adam Curtis's documentary called *The Power of Nightmares* to build support for swift and violent revenge for the most violent attack on metropolitan America since Pearl Harbour. We forget now how confused we all were about the difference between the Taliban and Al-Qaeda, and that, for many Americans, Osama bin Laden and Saddam Hussein were, if not the same person, at least the twin heads of the same empire of evil. We forget too, with the passage of time, quite how events unfolded and in what order. How the universal outrage at the attacks on the Twin Towers lead to the invasion of Afghanistan in 2001. How that campaign was quietly forgotten as the Bush Administration shifted its focus to its old enemy in Iraq. The gradual ramping up of pressure over Iraq in 2002 and the increasingly frantic attempts by Tony Blair to try to persuade Bush to build a wide coalition over Iraq as he had in Afghanistan and to follow the UN route. And then in March 2003 the huge march for peace contrasting with the dash for war before the summer heat made it impossible. The shock of the initial attack giving way to the shock and disappointment of the looting and the violence. The spiral of unintended consequences and the publication of the Iraq Survey Group report in 2004 revealing that there were no WMD after all. The accusations of deliberate lying over the intelligence used to justify the war and the endless and unsatisfying public inquiries.

But, if we forget how we felt then, we also see better the mistakes we made. Now, to most non-Americans at least, the idea of declaring war on 'terror' looks as absurd as declaring war on evil, or on war itself. As America's recessional from its quasi-imperial misadventures in Iraq and Afghanistan gathers pace, we see the utter folly of invading not one but two Muslim lands without knowing either what you were getting into, or how you were going to get out – all the while doing little or nothing about the Israel-Palestine dispute, the central issue between Islam and the West, and one of the sources of the anger that has fed the atrocities committed by Al-Qaeda.

Up until the General Election of June 2001, I had a ringside view of the Blair Government as Principal Private Secretary to the then Foreign Secretary, the late Robin Cook. After that election, Tony Blair replaced Cook with Jack Straw, and I went as Ambassador to Israel. Both in London and later in Tel Aviv I saw the most secret intelligence – which came in sealed plastic envelopes – which suggested that Saddam had WMD. Unlike Robin Cook, who told the House of Commons in his remarkable resignation speech on 18 March 2003, that Saddam probably did not have WMD in the commonly accepted sense of the term, I thought that he was likely to have such weapons. I based that judgement on the intelligence I was shown, much of which was later shown to be either false or misleading.

But, like Robin Cook, I did not see that Saddam's possession of WMD justified invading his country in the absence of support from the UN, from the EU or from NATO, without a sound basis in international law. Nor did I see how we were going to put Iraq back together again once we had taken it apart. Or why, when the policy of containment had worked, we couldn't give inspections more time. I believed that the real reasons for the fact and the timing of the invasion lay in American domestic politics, not the realities of the Middle East.

As an official serving abroad, I was spared the agonies of those in Whitehall who knew – deep down – that the invasion was morally wrong, politically mad, and almost certainly illegal. But only two serving officials – Elizabeth Wilmshurst (the Foreign Office deputy legal adviser) and Carne Ross (a young diplomat who had worked on Iraq at the UN) – had the guts to go. The rest stayed on, salving their consciences by telling themselves that, once Ministers had taken their decision, it was their duty to serve. Only recently a former very senior official discussed the events of 2003 with me, still twisting himself into knots eight years on, arguing that he hadn't resigned because he had believed that invading Iraq had been illegitimate, but not actually illegal.

History has shown that he and so many of the rest of us should have known better. Invading Iraq in the way we did and when we did was the most disastrous mistake in British – and probably American – foreign policy in a generation.

As Sarah Helm's play reminds us so painfully, what compounded the agony of the initial catastrophic error was the discovery not only that Saddam had no weapons of mass destruction (as Robin Cook had warned the House of Commons on the eve of invasion) but that the intelligence suggesting that he had had such weapons was false or fabricated.

Naturally the details of the play's plot are fiction, and have to be, not least for legal reasons. But that should not obscure the deeper truths about deceit, both wilful and wishful, at the highest levels of government which the play sets out, so graphically.

Reliving all those arguments through this play is agony, but a necessary one. It is an essential part of coming to terms with an especially traumatic episode in Britain's recent past.

But what made the play for me is more personal. Fundamentally it is a love story. A story of how two individuals, deeply committed to each other, but with profoundly different views on the central issue of the time, somehow keep going through it all. They are passionate about their professional engagements, as a journalist and as a public servant, but also about building their life, and that of their young family, together.

The demands of the children put all else in its proper perspective, and serve only to highlight the vanities and vacuities of high politics. The children's splashing subversive presence offstage is the counterpoint to the central business of the drama, but also its true context.

The first and last question most people will ask about *Loyalty* will be 'Is it true?' Only Sarah Helm herself can answer this. But my guess is that *Loyalty* must be at once true, and not true, and somewhere in-between. Not everything in it can be literally true – it is not a documentary – though many or most of the details are remarkably accurate. Paradoxically, however, it uses fiction to get at some much deeper truths, about the reality of the Iraq war, and about how human beings relate to each other.

As Matthew Arnold pointed out in *Dover Beach*, as ignorant armies clash by night on darkling plains, in the end all we have is love. And that, in my personal view, is the exhilarating – and alarming – message at the heart of this work of understated power and fine-pointed passion.

Sherard Cowper-Coles's memoir of his time as Britain's Afghan envoy, Cables from Kabul, *has just been published by HarperPress.*

Hampstead Theatre is one of the U.K's leading new writing companies. Throughout its long history, the Theatre has supported a thriving local, national and international playwriting culture.

We commission plays in order to enrich and enliven this culture. We support, develop and produce the work of new writers, emerging writers, established writers, mid-career writers and senior writers and have a proud tradition for creating the conditions for their plays and careers to develop.

The list of playwrights who had their early work produced at Hampstead Theatre and who are now filling theatres all over the country and beyond include Mike Leigh, Michael Frayn, Brian Friel, Terry Johnson, Hanif Kureishi, Simon Block, Abi Morgan, Rona Munro, Tamsin Oglesby, Harold Pinter, Shelagh Stephenson, debbie tucker green, Crispin Whittell, Roy Williams and Dennis Kelly.

In January 2010, Edward Hall was appointed Artistic Director of Hampstead Theatre. His inaugural season was a box office success culminating in two West End transfers: Mike Leigh's *Ecstasy* (Duchess Theatre) and the Hampstead Downstairs production *Belongings* (Trafalgar Studios 2). The Daily Telegraph praised Hall for 'imaginatively restoring Hampstead Theatre's reputation as one of the liveliest venues in London', 27 June 2011.

Hall opened **Hampstead Downstairs** which stages raw, edgy and experimental work. The space intimately seats 90 people. Since its opening in November 2010, previous productions include *small hours* directed by Katie Mitchell, *.45* written by Gary Lennon, *The Stock Da'wa* directed by Kathy Burke, written by David Eldridge and *Belongings* written by Morgan Lloyd Malcolm.

Hampstead Theatre's new autumn and spring season 2011/2012 will continue to delight, inspire and engage with such directors as Katie Mitchell, Richard Eyre and Roger Michell taking to the stage.

Characters

Others

DECORATORS

MERVIN, a Home Office technician

DINERS

JIM, a journalist

Setting

The play is in two acts.

The first act takes place at Nick and Laura's home
in Stockwell, and begins in early 2003,
immediately before the outbreak of the Iraq War

The second act takes place at
Number Ten Downing Street in September 2004

Note

This play is a work of fiction.

This Hampstead Theatre production of *Loyalty* was first performed at Hampstead Theatre, London, on 14th July 2011. The cast and creative team was as follows:

TONY: Patrick Baladi
TOM / GEORGE / PETE VOICEOVER: Stephen Critchlow
MARISIA / SWITCH VOICE: Anna Koval
NICK: Lloyd Owen
LAURA: Maxine Peake
C / RUPERT / ALASTAIR: Michael Simkins
JAMES / AMERICA MILITARY VOICE: Colin Stinton

Creatives:
Writer: Sarah Helm
Director: Edward Hall
Designer: Francis O'Connor
Lighting Designer: Ben Ormerod
Sound Designer: Paul Groothuis
Costume: Caroline Hughes
Casting: Gabrielle Dawes CDG
Assistant Director: Oliver Rose
Production Manager: Dominic Fraser

LAURA: *(Narrating.)* The first time I met him – soon after the election – I'd gone in to Number Ten for a dinner and was waiting for Nick in the outer office, when he suddenly appeared in jogging pants, and said hello. He'd just been working out he said, and looked at me.

(Pause.)

Then he asked if I'd like to go upstairs to see the state apartments before dinner. So I said yes, of course, and he took me up. As he'd invited me I expected him to chat a little or tell me about the paintings or something. Anything! But he just stood there, silent, leaning against the marble mantelpiece and watched me as I wandered round. I mean stared really. I felt I should say congratulations on winning the election but I couldn't find the words. We were there quite some time. I felt scrutinised in some way and awkward – overdressed. The body language was – I don't know. Like he was checking me out.

After that he just arrived in our lives – and there were suddenly three of us in the relationship.

The phones never stopped. At first he'd call up himself. 'Hi err… is he around… yeah great…' no 'sorry to bother you' or anything – but why would he? And he soon learned to use 'Switch' as a cut-out and then it was 'Got the boss here for him. OK Laura? How're those babies?' That's Dot.

And so I got to know him – in a second-hand sort of way. Through osmosis mostly – listening to the answers to the questions he asked. Eavesdropping on calls he made to others. Hearing what was bothering him every hour of the day and night – Ecclestone broke on Hampstead Heath, Diana on Eggerdon Hill, Cheriegate, somewhere on Mont Blanc.

We even had him – and Gordon – at my bedside when I went into labour – talking about the Euro.

And he was always with us in the car – a voice hanging somewhere over the dashboard, asking for words on… the OTRs – the what? The first Mandelson resignation lasted all the way up the M1. Riveting.

13

Of course, the closer to the truth you are, the less you can reveal – so I couldn't write about it then. Besides, we were all in it together – a joint project – and for a while we got on pretty well.

But now it's started to feel – overcrowded. And I'm beginning to wonder how long the three of us can carry on.

Act One

March 2003.

Stockwell.

NICK and LAURA's bedroom.

There are signs of building work going on in the bedroom, including a stepladder and red boxes piled up by a wall. There are saucepans on the floor, and a toaster on a bedside table.

It is late in the evening. LAURA can be heard through a second door running a bath with children's noises. NICK is lying on the bed in jeans taking papers out of an open red box and flicking through them. The football is on a small TV with volume on low, but he isn't watching it. A pile of papers suddenly falls from his lap and he tries to pick them up, looking for somewhere to put them.

NICK: *(Tired, shouting through to the bathroom.)* Laura!

   (To himself.) Bloody chaos.

   Why've we got a toaster on my bedside table? *(Picks up a jar, finds it's sticky.)* Marmalade.

LAURA: The builders were in the kitchen today, sorry.

NICK: I can't find anything in all this – mess. And there was no hot water this morning. I hope you know what you've taken on here with this project of yours.

   A phone on a chest of drawers suddenly rings. He watches it but doesn't try to answer it. It stops after four rings. Then a mobile on the desk starts ringing and jumping around in a different ringtone. That also stops after four rings. NICK (who knows what is going to happen) now puts his hand over another mobile on the bed beside him. When this one starts to ring he puts it to his ear and talks.

(His talking-to-TONY voice.) Hi. Yeah. I'm in on that. Ten minutes right? *(Looks at watch.).* And I've made some changes to the UN draft. For Monday yes. We have to pin him down on that.

What? *(Starts flicking the TV remote.)* One-nil at half-time. No I don't know who scored. I can't believe you don't have Sky Sports. *(Pause; looks around.)* No. I don't live in the lap of luxury, as it happens.

I live in a terraced house in Stockwell, as I've told you before. Yes, that's right, near the Oval. Yep.

Puts phone down.

LAURA: *(Coming out.)* Look. It'll be worth it. I promise. We'll have space, at last. I feel we've got so – on top of each other. Now we'll be able to breath. A place for me to write in the new conservatory. And your new study *(Looks at the pile of papers.)* with your own secure phone line so I don't have to hear it all any more.

NICK: You don't have to hear it. You choose to hear it. When I let you.

LAURA: Well. I don't want to from now on. I've decided. Life's all too muddled up.

Goes back to bathroom.

NICK: Look I have to listen to a secure call right now. Where've you put the Brent?

From the bathroom, splashing noises, yelps.

LAURA: Top of the cupboard I think.

(Comes back in.) Must be important.

(Looks at her watch. Yawns.) Who is it then?

NICK: George.

LAURA: Oh? *(Half joking.)* Can't you tell him to ring back in the morning? We've got to look at some tiles.

She goes back to the bathroom.

NICK climbs on the stepladder to reach the top of the wardrobe to get a box containing his special secure phone. As he pulls it down a whole pile of clothes tumble down with it. During the following conversation LAURA is picking up the clothes and piling them back in the wardrobe while NICK is unpacking the special 'Brent' phone. The wire won't stretch to the chair so he sits on the floor next to her desk. Tries to fix something. Looks uncomfortable.

LAURA: *(Coming out of the bathroom again, now holding a towel.)* Can I listen?

NICK: I thought you'd lost interest...

LAURA: But this is different... he's going to tell George he's changed his mind right? He's not going to go all the way. That's what he said in his note.

NICK: What note?

LAURA: Found it under the bed, crippled myself trying to get it. Here it is. *(Takes a scrap of paper out of back pocket.)*

NICK: Give it back. It's mine.

LAURA: *(Holding on to it.)* Hey you agreed we don't have secrets at home.

NICK: What is it?

LAURA: Looks like a love letter from Tony to someone called George, which you've scrawled all over.

Looks up at him puzzled. He tries to snatch it again.

Let's see... Camp David and then Tony's written 'I'll be with you whatever' and you've crossed that out and written *(Trying to read writing.)* 'you can count on me whatever' which is very cunning isn't it because it could mean anything. I mean count on him to do what exactly?

He surely can't count on him if there's no second resolution, right?

NICK: Look I don't know.

LAURA: So – why write a note if he's going to speak to him?

NICK: Because it might help us get through to him. He doesn't always get the message.

LAURA: Oh.

Phone rings. NICK answers.

NICK: Two minutes? OK. *(Puts phone down.)* Shit. I have to get this working.

LAURA: So what are we going to say to George tonight? I mean does Tony think he can get him to wait for a second UN resolution?

NICK: Not sure.

NICK leaves the room.

LAURA: But you're always sure what he's thinking. You say that to survive at all you have to know what he's thinking preferably before he's even thinking about it – and to know what he's decided even when he's saying the opposite. So what's he thinking?

No answer. He obviously can't hear.

LAURA starts picking up the clothes that have fallen out of the cupboard.

(Narrating.) We even get his stuff here. These are his shirts. Cast-offs. With the sweat marks too *(Looks at label.)* Paul Smith this month.

You see he just spends so much time with him – first thing, still dressing, then he comes back here at night straight from the bedroom where they've been talking while Tony changes. So, he comes home with a sense... a smell, almost, of him about him. And he'll even give me the line of the day – if I let him.

I pick up all sorts of curious things about him too. He loves *The Simpsons*. Once told George to call back when it was on.

Drizzles oil on his toast for breakfast. Never passes the ball at football, and only plays tennis with his coach. It's sliced back-hand volleys this week.

(Picking up a scruffy pair of shoes.) Buys all his shoes at Churches. He's fanatical about shoes.

And he hates clutter – doesn't even read the papers unless someone puts a cutting in his box. I once let on to him that I'd read something about him in *Private Eye* and he turned to me and said 'Laura really! You don't read that do you?' As if somehow it was me who came from Mars and not him.

Pause. Looks at note.

Now I know he writes little billets-doux to George.

NICK: *(Coming back in fast with a spanner.)* I do know what he's thinking – but not what he's going to do. He hasn't decided yet. Everyone thinks he has. But he hasn't. He'll wait till the last minute to decide. Always does. It's muscle memory, he says.

LAURA looks puzzled.

Means you can alter the angle of the volley at the very last minute.

NICK tries a sliced backhand volley. LAURA looks mystified.

NICK: What do you think he's going to do?

LAURA: He's got to insist on UN support surely. At least you've given him a way out with this 'count on him' thing right? So George knows now we're not 'with him whatever'. Do you think Tony should send another note to make sure George understands the difference?

Doorbell rings loudly. LAURA looks at her watch.

Boxes?

NICK: Tom said he'd be late with them tonight.

MARISIA: *(Echoing him outside.)* Boxes. I'll go.

LAURA: Thanks Marisia.

MARISIA: Thanks Tom. Bye.

LAURA: *(Narrating.)* And he only has one box at weekends. We get two a night.

NICK's phone rings again.

NICK: One minute. OK *(Looks at watch, puts phone down.)* Shit.

NICK goes back to fiddling with plugs and doesn't respond.

MARISIA enters with two heavy red boxes. Looks for somewhere to put them and then heaves them onto the bed and leaves the room, but LAURA shouts after her and she comes back in.

LAURA: Marisia!

I just wanted to say thanks for helping the children with the banners. They look great. Show them to Nick. *(Winks.)*

NICK: Ouch.

MARISIA comes back in carrying Stop the War banners, spelt Wore. NICK laughs in his 'Hah' sort of laugh.

LAURA: Why don't you come too Marisia? Come on.

MARISIA: Me? Really? Well yes, OK. Can I? You won't mind will you Nick?

NICK: No. Please. Go ahead. Be my guest.

LAURA: Leaving at nine then. There'll be a heck of a crowd.

MARISIA: They're saying two million on the website.

Loud splashing noises.

I'll go.

MARISIA goes to the bathroom to help the children.

LAURA: So he might still tell George he's pulling out if there's no second resolution?

MARISIA: Can't turn the tap off.

LAURA: Just… turn it the other way.

NICK: They can't refuel without our bases.

LAURA: But he's told him he can't count on him… it might be… off… altogether. Even now? Thank God.

More splashing noises.

NICK: I hope the bloody mute is going to work this time.

'DRRR, DRRR' the Brent phone (very antiquated in appearance) suddenly rings, making a very loud, deep, throaty noise, giving both a start. He presses something and the noise stops. Fumbles with an earpiece. LAURA watches then looks for the second earpiece in the box and puts it in. We hear the call. Crackling. Two or three distant American voices talking on the line. Then:

AMERICAN MILITARY VOICE: Mr Prime Minister. We have the President of the United States for you.

TONY: *(To GEORGE. Faltering at start as lots of crackling.)* Hi. Hi. Are you there? Oh hi. How are you?

Sounds pleased to hear from him but both men talk awkwardly, particularly at first. TONY's voice sounds closer than GEORGE's. Almost as if he's in the bedroom with us. Can hear his intakes of breath, whereas GEORGE seems miles away. And there is a time lag across the Atlantic.

GEORGE: I'm fine, but, hey, more important how are *you*?

TONY: I'm very well. I'm very well, really.

GEORGE: Yeah. *(Laughs.)* You're looking good. So courageous. Your body language. Truly, I watched you on TV.

TONY: Yeah well. It's hard sometimes. Believe me. And you're doing pretty well yourself.

GEORGE: What me? I'm just ready to kick ass.

Lots of laughter.

LAURA and NICK glance at each other.

Shrieking from the bathroom.

TONY: *(A little embarrassed.)* Yeah well. But you know what's worrying me is the French. Chirac's behaviour is absurd.

GEORGE: Hey, what did the French ever do for anyone? What wars did they win since the French revolution?

TONY: Yeah, right. Right.

A child screams that the tap won't turn off. Sense of bathroom beginning to flood.

NICK holds the earpiece closer. LAURA goes out and comes back.

MARISIA comes in.

MARISIA: Pliers? I need pliers.

NICK gets up and passes them to her.

TONY: But did you hear that Portuguese guy? Really great. Gave it to them straight.

Lots of crackling.

That Portuguese guy.

GEORGE: Yeah? He did?

TONY: So... err, where do you think we go from here?

LAURA touches the earpiece.

GEORGE: We'd like to do the second resolution Friday.

NICK shakes his head. Mouthing 'No'.

Condi and Colin want to do it Friday. You know why – because we've got to move to closure on this. I can call in the chips with Chile.
There's a moment to do this and we're peaking nicely. But we need to close it down soon.

Pause. Crackle. NICK and LAURA both bend over, closer. There should be a sense here that this is a crucial moment, and NICK and LAURA should look as if they think they are influencing events.

TONY: Yeah.

Pause.

Well let me explain how I see it. We think Monday might be better.

LAURA is nodding, encouraging TONY. NICK is dead still.

I want to take the Europeans with me if I can. So Friday might be a little early for us.

Long silence from GEORGE. Distant talking. Crackling. TONY breathing. Then change of subject.

Any idea what game Putin's playing?

GEORGE: Oh yeah the Russians… well.
But you know the Germans have got some really good new stuff showing he has those biological weapons. You've seen that right?

NICK looks puzzled and LAURA looks towards him. They both hold the earphones closer.

TONY: Well, just heard something today. The Germans have a new source. Yeah. Sounded really convincing.

GEORGE: Y'know, the German stuff shows that son of a bitch is really ready to offload. No doubts now Tony.

TONY: No. Right. I got that too – from Berlin. Yeah. Great stuff.

Pause. Crackling. TONY breathing. MARISIA appears soaked from head to toe and pointing at the pliers. Obviously needs help. LAURA follows her out.

GEORGE: And y'know what? We should put a bug in on this and make sure Chirac gets to hear it. That would show him! (Loud laughs.)

23

And we can fix this thing. The Europeans are weak as hell but the Arabs are right with us on this now. Jordan, Bahrain. Even Mubarak.

TONY: Yeah but we can't allow Blix a veto.

GEORGE: Blix? What? That no-count.

Splashing noises. Children shrieking.

TONY: What? Oh Yeah, well.

GEORGE: But I'm really calling in the chips now. And with the Mexicans. Screw them down.

More shrieks of delight.

MARISIA: *(Shouting.)* Stop that. Stand still. This is horrible.

LAURA comes back, soaked. Picks up earpiece and starts listening again while signalling to NICK that he has to go out and help in the bathroom. He signals that he can't.

TONY: And, the fact of the matter is, we have to make people understand that we are not going to war because we want to, but because there is no alternative. It's our – duty – to do this thing.

GEORGE: Yes I have a big speech tomorrow and I'll put some words in on that.

TONY: Yeah great.

GEORGE: And I have to do something about my body language. But your body language is great. How do you do it?

TONY laughs.

And you know these polls, they are so unrealistic. If you ask people a question like do you want to go to war or would you rather have peace, they say peace. I mean it's absurd.

TONY: Yeah. Right. *(More nervous laughter.)*

GEORGE: That's your moral high ground. I mean do these people not care about the citizens of Iraq? The answer is no. But when that son-of-a-bitch hits Europe they'll be saying where were George and Tony?

TONY: Right. *(Nervous laughter.)*

Sound of something falling over and crashing from the bathroom. NICK and LAURA look up.

GEORGE: But you know Tony the American people will never forget what you're doing. And people say to me, you know, is Tony really with you all the way? Do you have faith in him. And I say yes because I recognise leadership when I see it. And true courage.

TONY: Well you're pretty courageous yourself George.

GEORGE: Look... err... I'll try and put it in your comfort zone Tony. We don't want regime change in London before we have it Iraq now do we?

TONY: Right.

Crackling breathing.

GEORGE: I have to cut this short now as I'm heading down to Texas but you can reach me there over the weekend if you need to talk.

TONY: Oh George, just one thing, and I know you think I keep banging on about this, but on the road map thing... if you can give us anything on Israel-Palestine it...

GEORGE: Oh yeah, sure, but gotta hop now. So catch you later.

Pause.

TONY: Yeah, bye George.

MARISIA comes out, soaked and obviously panicking, signals that NICK should go to the bathroom to help. He throws down the earpiece, which leaves LAURA still listening alone.

GEORGE: Oh and Tony. Don't forget – cojones.

LAURA looks puzzled. Line goes dead.

Pause. LAURA still with earpiece in looking towards the bathroom. Noises still coming out.

Then suddenly.

SWITCH: I have the Prime Minister for you coming through now on this line. BEEP BEEP.

TONY: Well what now? Do you think he'll hold off till next week?

LAURA: Let's hope so or… it's going to be a bloody mess. *(Silence.)* Oh err sorry. It's me. Hi. Err… I'll get Nick he's… he's… dealing with a flood. He'll call you back.

She puts phone down a little embarrassed. NICK comes back soaked from head to toe.

(To NICK.) I said you'd call him back.

(Going to the bathroom, muttering.) Roadmaps… miracles. Oh my God. The mess.

(Shouting back to NICK.) He's just using you can't you see?

NICK: *(Sits at desk. Calls SWITCH. As he waits at the desk he stares at laptop and appears to be scrolling down something, emails maybe.)* Bloody hell!… Laura… I can't believe you're doing this. What are you doing having lunch with your old boyfriend? At a time like this.
Yeah I'll hold.

LAURA: *(Now drying in the bathroom.)* What?

NICK: Jim Johnson? Orsos?

She obviously doesn't hear. He waits. Types something in and presses what would appear to be the send button. Then shouts.

You've just cancelled.

LAURA walking back in with a towel round her head.

He's just using you. Look!

LAURA: What? I can't believe you're reading my emails.

Snatches laptop, half joking, hides it under a towel and takes it back to the bathroom.

NICK: You listen to my phone calls. What do you see in him? Writing such tripe.

Hears bathroom door bang.

LAURA: *(Coming back out.)* Well at least he's been to Iraq – unlike some people. I mean what's got into you? You know I like to keep in touch with my old friends. Find out what they're picking up – and what they're not.

NICK: What do you two talk about?

LAURA: Why do you suddenly want to know? Anything. What we want to talk about. The weather!

NICK: *(Suddenly, unexpectedly, losing his cool. Turning cold/angry and standing up.)* What you learn at home is not a fucking story Laura. It's not some… great scoop you've gone out and dug up to splash over the newspapers. It's our life. And what do you do with these notes? *(Picks up a notebook, feels something sticky.)* Bloody marmalade.

LAURA: *(Coming out of the bathroom. Shocked by sudden aggression. Silent for a minute.)* Look! You have your friends. I have mine. And I talk to them when the hell I like, thank you very much. Especially now. I can't write what I think any longer. Now I can't even say what I think.
Is that it? What do you expect?

She starts back to the bathroom.

NICK: *(Quietly/testily/sarcastic. Looks at her.)* Loyalty. Shall I spell it for you?

Long pause.

She turns, is speechless. Looks at him in total disbelief.

LAURA: You sounded just like your father for a minute then.

He backs off now.

NICK: Look. You've always known that this whole thing doesn't work between us if I can't trust you.

It's just that it's… someone's been leaking stuff… Nothing much. Just tittle tattle. But…

LAURA: What did you say? Leaking?

MARISIA crosses back and forth with towels. NICK waits for her to go through before saying, lowering his voice.

NICK: It's dangerous Laura. He's dangerous. Especially now. He has an agenda. You know that.

LAURA: Now hang on. *(Also trying to keep her voice down.)* You're going to bomb thousands of innocent people any day now and… and… you're telling me it's dangerous to go to lunch at Orsos? Jim is a friend. He and I were writing about Saddam before you'd even heard the word Halabja. And how dare you accuse me of leaking stuff. I hope someone is. They bloody well should be. Robin must be. And that woman who resigned the other day? At least she had some guts. You just can't see straight any more. Talking of which you've put the wrong washer on that… tap. You're just… pathetic. I'm going to resign – even if you're not.

She goes back into the bathroom. Bangs the door. Comes straight out again.

(Suddenly totally losing her cool.) Look, I sit here day in day out buried in book proofs and builders' dust and now look they've completely screwed up the plumbing because you couldn't even find time to fix a simple washer for me. And what about some loyalty to me? I mean to us? To how we see the world. To what we thought mattered. Or did. Once. I am not one of those wives who…

NICK: We're not married.

LAURA: …who stands by her husband while he screws the bloody country…

Pause.

And thank God we aren't married.

Throws a towel at him and he ignores it.

You'd have gone all the way 'whatever' to Hitler's bunker would you?
Or might you have had the guts to pull out at Wannsee?
I mean here we are painting the house in Celadon blue and you're about to smash a whole country to smithereens just because that man *(Pointing to the phone.)* wants to kick someone's 'ass'. He just said so. Right here. Let's call off the builders. Save the taxpayer some money.

NICK: How on earth?

LAURA: Because at least Mervin won't have to bombproof the glass. I couldn't see how he could stick film over the new regency architrave anyhow.

NICK: Well he won't have to. Home Office says I've dropped down the hit list.

LAURA: What? Now? *(Laughs.)* But I thought we were all about to be bombed in 45 minutes. And poisoned by a million anthrax spores. Well good old Mervin. At least he's got some intelligence.

She goes into bathroom briefly but he doesn't notice.

NICK: Meant to tell you he's coming on Saturday to downgrade the alarm. But we can keep the Car Bomb Alarm and the panic buttons apparently. Hang on isn't Saturday Harry's birthday party? Did we book the magician? *(Looks at diary.)* March 15th, shit. I'll be in the Azores for this silly summit. *(Looks in diary again.)*
You know, if war breaks out I'll have to cancel my climbing in the Alps. Again.

Pause.

Maybe it's time we did get married. What do you think?
Honeymoon in the Pyrenees perhaps? *(Looking up but she's
not there. Then she comes out of the bathroom.)*

LAURA: Panic buttons. So at least we can still be shot.

NICK: What?

LAURA: Remember he said panic buttons are only any use
if you're about to be finished off with a shot to the head,
usually by the bed. You're usually flat out on the floor by
then which is why the buttons are always at ground level.

(Pause. She's looking for her notebook. Tries to move boxes off the bed.)

Anyway *(Calming down.)* what is that new German source
the Americans have suddenly produced? At the eleventh
hour? Sounded a little desperate. Didn't it? You just have
to listen to them talk – to know – to feel – how they're
deluding themselves. I don't believe in him. This German
source.

*She picks up notebook and starts writing in it. NICK staring at
screen saying nothing.*

NICK: You don't?

LAURA: No I don't.

Sounded like a – put-up job of some sort. Like a – ploy or
a plant. Or something. I'm going to leak that entire phone
call.

NICK: *(Looking at her. Friendlier.)* You can't. Nobody would
believe it.

LAURA: *(Calming, doesn't hear him.)* Clutching at straws. I feel –
disgusted by it all. Ashamed. Really. I long for everyone to
hear what I hear. Then they'd know how it really is. But as
I can't tell anyone I don't want to hear any more. It sickens
me. I feel like throwing up.

NICK: So what would you have said to George then, if it's so
easy?

Look. Listen. Tony thinks he can still influence the
Americans. He thinks he has to stay close to them – and
then there's a chance they'll listen. It's – risky – but he has
to make them think he's with them all the way, even if he
isn't.

LAURA: Yes. And what did Clinton say last night? *(Picks up
notebook, looks in it.)* Here. 'George is making you swallow
a turd'.

Pause.

NICK: I have to be supportive. Or else I'll…

LAURA: …you'll have no influence either. But perhaps it's a
trap and we're all going to have to swallow Clinton's turd.
And you won't even tell me what you're thinking any
more. You only tell him. You're back later and later every
night.

NICK: You sound jealous.

LAURA: I think you're spending too much time with him. He's
a – bad influence.

Can't you find a new friend?…

NICK: Look if he didn't trust me I'd have no leverage at all
and there'd be no way of…

LAURA: Stopping it. Right? So although you say you don't
to him – you do want to stop it. Just like me. I know you
don't really believe in it so why don't you just come on the
march with me? Then – after that we could get married.
That would be nice.

NICK: Why will you never understand? *(Reaches out to her.)*

Landline rings.

LAURA: It's him.

NICK: *(To SWITCH.)* OK. Hi. Yeah hi.
(In his speaking-to-TONY voice.) Yeah sorry about that.
Something more urgent came up. Yes. Marisia did.
Plumbing course at Bialystock high school. Yes but don't
you worry I'll dry out.
Yes they are 3-3 at extra time.
Maybe a week, maybe less. You had a note from me on it
in your box.
Yeah. I thought so too. CDS called today on Diego Garcia.
But that German source George mentioned was news to
me. Seemed a bit odd. Why bring that up now? We – I
thought it sounded a bit like he was – *(Looks at LAURA.)*
clutching at straws. Didn't it?

(Long pause/listening.) Err…right. OK. Well I'm sorry. I
didn't know.

*LAURA pacing around. Stops suddenly picking up new tone from
NICK. Listens carefully.*

From C?

Long pause as he listens.

I see.

(NICK gets up and starts pacing phone in hand.) No? Today?
You saw C today? *(Raises his voice.)* OK. OK. I'm sorry. I
didn't know. Nobody told me. A meeting? Where? When?
After the JIC?
Obviously.
And so this is the same source George was talking about
you think?
Was it just the two of you? OK. Nobody else in there? Yes,
yes of course you can see who you like.
When you like.
OK, sure he delivers. I know he talks straight. But he has
his… agenda. Of course you can. It's just that I mean I
think you need someone in there with you. Especially now.
He's – well – it's risky.
You just have to be aware of the limitations of this stuff. It
isn't always quite what it seems.

Said he could find them in time. Oh he did did he? Well
that would certainly come in very handy right now.
Daisy? What?
Oh I see. Well you'd better – err – not say any more. We're
not on the secure line now.
What?
(Starts flicking the TV remote.) No don't even look at the
press summary. Jim Johnson? Utter crap as usual *(Looking
at LAURA.)* Here you are 4-3 to them on a penalty shoot
off – OK shoot out. Well use Alastair for your football
commentary.
You can claim it on expenses now you know.

*Puts the landline down. NICK now gets down on the floor to pack
up the 'Brent' telephone. Seems very tired, anxious. Puts it back in
the box. And then back in the cupboard. Closes the cupboard door.
Looks agitated. Muttering. Then he goes over to his red boxes. Heaves
out large pile of papers.*

LAURA: *(Gets the tile brochure out.)* You know it's great to know
we still agree on some things. That you haven't moved to
Mars too. *(Pause.)* What about Turquoise Foxglove? And
– I know it's what you believe – it must be. It can't not be –
or else… It would once have been.

NICK: I can't believe he's doing this.

LAURA: What? What? What's he doing?

NICK: Oh nothing. He's so… sly sometimes.

LAURA: What? It's him isn't it, who's rattling you. Not me. It's
just I get the flak.

NICK: Just leaving me out of such an important meeting. At
this time. It's just… Seeing C like that. On his own. He's
been seeing him on his own.

LAURA: So? That must happen all the time doesn't it? He is
the Prime Minister after all. He's a free agent… like me.

NICK: No. No it doesn't. He can't. Shouldn't. One of us must
be in there with him – to keep him grounded. It's the

oldest rule in the book. A PM is not supposed to see these intelligence guys on their own. It's… obvious. If Graham knew he'd hit the roof.

LAURA: Why? Because they can't understand all the gobbledegook. What?

NICK: He… he wants to hear stuff. And C knows he wants to hear it. Shit. I wonder if Graham does know.

LAURA: Call him. Let's call Graham now. Perhaps there's something we can still do to stop it. I'll get onto switch. Jesus Christ Nick this is really dangerous. There's still time. You said there was still time.

Picks up phone.

NICK: No. *(Snatches phone back. Still agitated. Pacing around.)* I don't like it. And there'll be absolutely no record either. Shit. Why didn't he tell me about this source? I wonder what the Germans are really saying – and to who?

LAURA: What exactly does cojones mean?

NICK: Balls.

She keeps flicking through the brochure.

Why?

LAURA: It was the last thing George said. *(She picks up notebook and makes a note.)*

NICK: Hah! It's his favourite word.

LAURA: But it was a little odd the way George brought it up wasn't it?

NICK: What? The intelligence from the Germans?

LAURA: Yes.

NICK: A bit. Yes.

LAURA: Why now? You've all been telling us for months in these dossiers that WMD's a certain fact. Is the certain fact now suddenly more certain? *(Pause.)* There isn't any real evidence on WMD is there? Just bits of old rumour. They put together the best story they could, right?

NICK: *(Hardening momentarily.)* A story every intelligence agency in the world believes. That the whole machinery of government believes.

LAURA: Emperor's clothes.

And look, here, *(Looks round, picks up a notebook.)* I found this interview I told you about. The one I did with that UN weapons inspector in Baghdad. A Fin. Very blonde. He said they'd destroyed the lot after the first Gulf War and there was no way Saddam could get them back. Look he gave me chapter and verse – a great long list, all blown up. So how did Saddam get them all back?

NICK: Give me a break.

LAURA: Well I'm only trying to help. Maybe it'll filter back through reverse osmosis somehow.

NICK: Err like, excuse me everyone but my wife doesn't believe it. She once went to Baghdad and met a Finnish bloke who said it wasn't true...

LAURA: Well I did. And I don't. But more important, nor do you. I know you aren't sure. And you are supposed to be. I can tell just looking at you. And I just feel it's all wrong.

Pause.

NICK: You just feel instinctively. In your gut. What use is that?

LAURA: Partly yes. And what's wrong with that? I think I'm picking it up somehow – from you maybe. Or through you. Kind of seeping through you to me – from him even. Is that possible? I mean it's your fault that I don't believe it. Because you don't. You're trying to because he wants you to. But you don't. Not really.

Looks at NICK who looks at her as if she's crazy.

Is it true? That there's no real evidence to speak of? *(Looks at him.)* Yes! It's really true. That's frightening.

Pause. Silence. Not really listening to her. Reading papers. She makes notes in her notebook.

LAURA: And I kind of – smell it. Maybe I've spent too long with the archives. Hundreds of crinkly notes marked official secret. You can see so clearly how the signals were hopelessly misread back then. You can spot the traitors – just conmen in it for the money often. And you want to shout back over the years and warn everyone 'Don't believe him. Stop! For God's sake don't do it'. Then they do. More agents dropped into Gestapo hands.

Pause.

This new German source of yours is probably just some smooth conman... some... waiter... I don't know from downtown Baghdad who's found his way to Germany and wants to make money with what he heard from a cousin of a brother of a friend back home.

She gets up and goes to her pile of papers. Pulls out a file.

Like this Frenchman with a quiff. Code name Onion. Recruited in 1941 in Paris, dirt track racing – fooled everyone in London and betrayed hundreds of British agents. All the warning signals ignored. It's quite clear looking back today but I wonder what it looked like then. What's your German source's code name, do you know?

Pause, silence.

NICK: Daisy.

LAURA: What?

NICK: He's called Daisy. Your Baghdad waiter's code name. It's Daisy.

LAURA: Daisy? *(Writes something in her notebook.)*

SCENE TWO

Stockwell kitchen a few days later. MARISIA and LAURA are preparing for a children's birthday party. Again, there are signs of building works. MARISIA is blowing up balloons. LAURA is icing a cake. MERVIN (in overalls) is also in the room, often on the floor, checking the alarm equipment. LAURA and MARISIA largely ignore him and the alarms going off.

Radio news is on in the background.

MERVIN's alarm goes off in a test. Beeping. Then it stops and the phones start ringing continuously for a moment.

LAURA looks towards the phones wondering whether to pick up. Then they suddenly stop.

LAURA: *(Narrating.)* Sometimes the phone calls stop – just like that. And we're suddenly cut off, perhaps for days. No explanation given.

Or Nick might come home, earlier than usual and complain that his door has been closed all day. No explanation for that either.

One time he came home and said 'I'm out tomorrow.'

Why? I said. Who says? It's been decided, he said. Some head has to roll. But why yours?

Goes with the job.

Then next day his door was open wide again and Nick was back in. We were all miraculously re-connected up.

Phones beep.

MARISIA: What time's the magician coming?

LAURA: Five I think.

MARISIA: Did you know he always carries a good luck charm?

LAURA: Who? The magician?

MARISIA: No! *(Loud laugh.)* Tony.

LAURA: I know he keeps crystals on his desk. Presents from Peter apparently.

MARISIA: And he carries the Koran around in his inside pocket. Just in case.

LAURA: In case of what?

MARISIA: Oh I don't know.

LAURA: You've got to know him pretty well too haven't you Marisia?

MARISIA: Only because Nick tells me things – when I make his sandwiches.

You know what I learned this morning. He doesn't think England is big enough. Long enough but not wide enough. So I said well tell him from me it's dangerous to think like that. I mean Hitler thought Germany wasn't big enough so he walked right into Poland.

LAURA: Yes. *(Looking at MARISIA who's now attaching balloons to the ceiling.)* Sandwiches? Since when have you been making sandwiches for Nick?

MARISIA: Since Tony stopped getting his delivered. Didn't you know? Tony used to get these really nice sandwiches brought in from Pret A Manger so Nick would get the leftovers, but now they have a 'guru' – is that the word? Carol they call her. And she's stopped the Pret delivery because Tony's not allowed wheat.

LAURA looks up at MARISIA, amazed, then carries on icing the cake.

I felt sorry for Nick because he hasn't got time to get out to the shops, with all this going on. He's obviously not eating properly. Haven't you noticed? And he told me had to fly to Belfast and back twice in one day last week just so he could squeeze the war cabinet in between. He looks exhausted. Don't you think?

LAURA: Does he? *(Anxious.)* And err what did Nick say when you said Tony was like Hitler?

Beep of MERVIN's alarm test drowns out the answer.

MARISIA: *(Now fixing a happy birthday sign.)* Do they have all that health food stuff at those dinners you go to round there? Must be horrible.

LAURA: Oh I don't really notice the food.

MARISIA: What's it like there?

LAURA: Oh like any other place, really – except not. Tony and Cherie were in bare feet last time. Cherie was sort of curled up on the sofa. 'Like family tonight isn't it Tony,' she said and looked at me.

MARISIA: Really. *(Laughs loud.)* And what did he say?

LAURA: Oh something about Nick. *(Laughs and sort of imitates TONY).* 'There are four people working well at the moment and he's one of them.'
'He is?' I said.
'Yeah really. He is. Isn't he Cherie? Couldn't do without him right now. Moving me on. Doesn't hang about does he? Is it like that at home?'

MARISIA: Always! He put the children's bags in the car the other day before I'd packed them.

LAURA: And I said 'you mean like starting the washing up before we've finished eating?'
And Tony said 'Does he do that? Really? He does the washing up then?'
'Yes but he always leave a soaking mess behind,' I said, thinking how on earth's he got me talking about the bloody washing up of all things?

MARISIA: Who do you sit next to?

LAURA: Oh he usually puts me next to him – which is really odd because he never seems to notice that I'm there.

Doorbell goes. LAURA looks at watch.

MARISIA: Boxes. I'll go.

LAURA: Oh Tesco – yes.

MARISIA goes out to get Tesco boxes.

LAURA: *(Alone narrating, except for MERVIN whose alarms beep during the story.)* I always try not to speak at these dinners because I – well, like one day they were attacking Clare as usual, saying how outrageous it was that she had complained about the tapping of Kofi's phone.

So I said 'But is it true? I mean was it true?' And everyone just looked at me open-mouthed. 'I mean, were they tapping his phone?' And he turned and stared at me a second and then said 'Oh Laura, really.' And I glanced at Nick but he just looked blank.

Once he started talking about Hebron which he'd just visited but he obviously hadn't been able to see a lot – driving through in a bullet proof car. So I told him about the first time I went there, to write about three Palestinians shot dead by Israeli undercover soldiers. I wanted to find the exact spot where it happened so my guide, Mazen, took me down a track to an open space where a group of young boys were staring up at a tree where three black plastic bags were hanging.

Pause.

Then one of the kids pointed at one of the bags and said the word 'Shahid' – martyr. Mazen nodded then whispered to me that the Israelis had taken away the bodies so the boys had scraped the remaining blood and guts off the ground and put it in the plastic bags and hung them on the tree. They needed some remains to honour.

Mazen started filming the little black bags. And I started staring at them too.

Pause.

Tony seemed to be listening closely. Then he said 'Yeah but – you know – we can find a solution out there.'

Then someone started talking about Gordon. Darth Vader.
And how he'd turned up that day with his Imperial Storm
troopers.

And one time when all the others were chatting amongst
themselves about Gordon, he suddenly seemed to
remember I was there and he turned to me specifically and
pointed at the chandelier – paused a moment – and with
the light full on his face he said 'The question is – should
I have done something? Should I have cut him off a long
time ago?'

I have no idea why he said that to me.

See you next time Mervin.

Final long beep. MERVIN leaves.

MARISIA now trying to find room for Tesco boxes, moving red boxes.

MARISIA: Wow. No room at all is there?

MARISIA sorts the delivery.

LAURA: The children won't notice the mess.

MARISIA: Not when the magician's here. I'll put stuff up here
for now. Oh no! *(Drops something on breakfast bar and a cloud
of icing sugar floats up.)* Sorry.

LAURA: No it's OK. *(Picking up a document shakes icing sugar off
it.)* You just iced the attorney general's report. *(Blows the
sugar off it. Laughs.)*

MARISIA: Well it's very boring. I read it this morning.

Is Nick coming to the party?

LAURA: He's flying back from the Azores. Says he'll stop off
on the way in from the airport.

MARISIA: Azores. What's that?

LAURA: A place he's been to talk about the war.

MARISIA: But there isn't going to be a war really.

LAURA: Martha next door thinks it's Armageddon. Tell your husband, she said. I said I don't have a husband.

Pause.

MARISIA: But Martha's right Laura. You should tell him. He listens to you. Perhaps you could get him to do something. You know? To stop it. Really. He respects you.

LAURA: Respects me?

MARISIA: Yes of course. And I thought you were going to get married sometime. No?

LAURA: You know my friends have started treating me like I've got an infectious disease or something.

Could you pass the candles.

MARISIA: What does Nick really think?

LAURA: I don't know any more Marisia. He's shutting down.

MARISIA: If you're not with us you're against us. Right. *(Laughs.)*

LAURA: *(Slight laugh.)* Why don't you ask him about the war Marisia. You'd probably get more out of him than me right now.

MARISIA: Oh I have asked. That's the problem. I asked him what he thought of the march we went on. All those people. He told me as many people were gassed by Saddam as marched in Hyde Park.

LAURA: It's exactly what Tony said in his statement. You're just getting the line. Like me.

MARISIA: *(Suddenly emotional/angry.)* But it made me mad the way he said it. The voice. Flat you know. I recognised it. I'm Polish. The Soviets gave us the line for all those years telling us they were good guys and the Nazis did all the killing. Then we learned what really happened. Katyn and all that. You know. Lying communists. Bloody murderers.

Phone rings.

LAURA: Here he is. *(Answering phone.)* Yes any minute Dot.

Door bangs.

NICK comes in with suits, suitcase, red boxes and enormous birthday present and flowers. Straight to the phone, trying to hold on to everything. MARISIA tries to help him.

NICK: *(To SWITCH.)* Yes. One minute.

Puts phone down. Turns radio on. Kisses LAURA.

LAURA: How were the Azores?

NICK: Ridiculous.

> Got a call. What time's the magician coming? I'll help you with that in a minute.

Runs upstairs. Minute later shouts down.

> Where the hell's the Brent?

LAURA: Down here. Had to empty the cupboard.

Runs back down. Finds it. Fixes it up.

LAURA: Who is it?

NICK: Only Kofi.

LAURA: Poor Kofi.

MARISIA: *(Looking at watch.)* Help. I'm late to collect the children. I'll stick the balloons on the door on the way out.

The Brent makes its loud ringing tone. NICK puts in an earpiece as he does the washing up and so does LAURA (as she does the icing).

VOICE: *(Crackling.)* I have the UN Secretary General for you Prime Minister.

KOFI: Hello Tony. Can you hear me?

TONY: Yes I hear you. It's going to have to be brief I'm afraid Kofi I've only just landed...

KOFI: Look Tony I won't take up too much of your time but I wanted to tell you… the atmosphere here is tense. We're not sure that tactics being used by certain Security Council members are helpful.

TONY: I see.

KOFI: Well I'm going to tell it to you straight here Tony. We have a public relations problem because there's no smoking gun out there. We don't think the case has been made out yet and we want Blix to keep looking. And I don't think you're going to get this second resolution through without more time. Can you use your influence?

TONY: Yeah Kofi, I hear what you say but, you know, they are out there. Somewhere. Iraq is a big place to hide things you know.

KOFI: I am asking for your support over this Tony. Too early and it could be a fatal blow for us.

TONY: Well you know my position, Kofi.

KOFI: *(Long pause. Deep sigh.)* Tony you're a courageous man. Let's stay in touch.

TONY: Yes of course Kofi. Let's stay in touch.

Phone goes down. LAURA leaves room. Landline rings.

NICK: OK. Yeah. Yeah – dickering around as usual.
What? Words on what? Err OK. Just hold on a minute.
Pity you don't do Google.

(Shouts to LAURA.) Laura. Could you look up Abyssinia League of Nations 1936?

LAURA: Why? Will it help? Will it help Kofi?

NICK: Yes. Now! Go on just do it. Please.

(To TONY.) We're… err… I'm digging something out.

LAURA: *(Sits at laptop.)* Abyssinia, Abyssinia crisis, here we go. School curriculum Year 6. 20th century heroes and villains.

NICK: *(Putting speaker phone on to LAURA.)* Read it.

(To TONY.) Hold on.

LAURA: This any good? Abyssinia, member of the League of Nations. October 1935, Mussolini attacks Abyssinia. League intervention too late. Delivered fatal blow to League of Nations. Was Mussolini an Italian hero leading his people to glory? Or was he an international bully... endangering world peace?
How's that?

NICK: How's that?

Pause.

TONY: Good. Should do the trick.

LAURA: Trick? What trick?

MARISIA: *(Shouting from outside the door.)* Laura, Nick come quick. It's horrible. Someone's smeared red paint all over the front door.

NICK and LAURA: What? What's happened?

MARISIA: 'War criminals'.

NICK: Bloody vandals.

Rushes out.

LAURA: What? Oh no. Get it off. Get it off. *(Distraught, standing holding wooden spoon with icing on it, shouting.)* Don't let the children see. Take them round the back. For God's sake, don't let the children see.

SCENE THREE

The Stockwell bedroom a few days later. LAURA is getting ready to go out. Looks different. More dressed up.

LAURA: *(Narrating.)* In the days before the war it fell strangely quiet at home. Nick was rarely here so we couldn't argue any more. I tried to go out as much as possible, to see what others were saying. But nobody was asking the right questions, or so it seemed to me.

Tanks were sent to Heathrow one day, and we weren't told why. Then we had a smallpox scare and then another plague of anthrax spores, and botulism arrived too. Tony told us that any of these poisons would cause 'excruciatingly painful death'. Those were his words. 'Excruciatingly painful'.

At one point a BBC reporter, called Andrew Gilligan, thought he'd got a scoop on the intelligence but instead he botched it up; and there were tragic consequences.

The landline rings. Then her mobile rings.

Hi.

Door bangs downstairs.

Err no. I'll have to ring you back.

Puts phone down. She types something on her laptop. Closes it. NICK comes in.

NICK: Who was that? Could you answer the landline?

LAURA: I'm going out.

NICK: Isn't it a bit late... *(Picks up phone.)* Hello Tom. Yes. OK. On the secure line? Are you sure. He thinks it's really necessary? OK give me a minute.

Puts phone down, starts setting up the Brent.

NICK: Where are you going?

LAURA: *(Trying different lipsticks.)* Out.

NICK: I can see that.

LAURA: There's some shepherd's pie in the fridge.

NICK: Thanks.

Anywhere nice?

Looks at the TV which is on.

Fucking BBC. Where are they getting that?

Switches it off.

LAURA: Why is the BBC always fucking nowadays? I like the BBC.

Switches it on again.

NICK: Is that new? You look different. Your hair or something. You've painted your nails.

Looks at her strangely.

She is about to leave but he offers her the earphones.

Phone goes. She listens.

NICK: OK yes. I'm here. Put him through.

PETE: *(Sinister, quite nervous sounding.)* This is a call that never happened. You'll understand Nick.

NICK: Yes I get lots of calls like that.

PETE: Not like this one you don't. It's very important. Not to beat about the bush, we've found him.

NICK: Really? You're sure it isn't another double?

PETE: No. No. Not Saddam. I mean we've found Gilligan's source.

NICK: Oh… right… right. *(Suppressing a nervous laugh at his error.)*

PETE: We'll call him in of course. Probably throw the Official Secrets Act at him. Section Two.

Pause.

We have no choice.

NICK: Can you say who it is?

PETE: A junior official – as we thought. Name's Kelly.

NICK: Kelly.

PETE: Too junior to have known anything. When the name comes out it'll show that Gilligan's story was rubbish. He had no real intelligence source at all.

NICK: I see. But why should the name come out... how...

PETE: Oh the name's around already and there's no way it can be kept quiet.

NICK: Really? But hang on a minute. We shouldn't give out the name we never give out these names – what if Gilligan had other sources.

PETE: Gilligan's a cunt.

Phone goes down. LAURA looks at NICK.

LAURA: Nice company you're keeping nowadays. Tony's Kommissars!

NICK: *(Looking at her strangely again.)* Whose company are you keeping?

LAURA: *(Putting on coat. Picking up bag.)* What does he mean – 'the name's going to come out?'
He's going to give out this Kelly's name isn't he?
Deliberately. He already has hasn't he? Just to rubbish the story. Scare others off. I bet he has.
Official Secrets obviously not enough any more so we're doing official smears as well.

NICK: No I am not.

LAURA leaves slamming the door.

SCENE FOUR

Stockwell bedroom a few days later. Late evening.

LAURA: *(Narrating.)* By the third week of March we were with the Americans 'whatever' – or so everyone seemed to think.

But here at home there was still a sense that options weren't all closed off. I can't explain that exactly. Perhaps

I was still picking up some signals from Nick. I noticed he hadn't cancelled his climbing holiday yet.

There was certainly a nervousness – that I remember. He called up late at night to talk about anything. Thatcher went round one evening.

I just felt that something could still shift out there. We were still waiting for a trigger. Then he'd decide – muscle memory – just like that.

There were a handful of doubters left in parliament, but he knew he could win them round. It was all down to his speech.

I'd seen from very close up how he did this. By chance I was standing right behind him once as he waited to go down the tunnel and out on to the Brighton stage. The thundering roar swirls around you in the darkness back there among the dusty staging and with his back to me, I could see him kind of limbering up for his keynote speech and shifting from foot to foot. Then the music, beating, reached a fever pitch, suddenly sucking him up out of the tunnel up towards the lights and there he was up there on the platform close to a giant sun, hanging from the scaffolding.

And he must have been blinded in the lights, and all those upturned faces were there right at his feet – lady ushers with earphones were gyrating madly and he glowed up there like a pop star – for a performance of – well, real brilliance.

Every face and body muscle straining to demonstrate – absolute conviction.

Looks at watch. Gets into bed. Reads.

Landline rings.

Oh hello Dot.

Door bangs downstairs.

(To NICK as he comes in.) It's Switch.

(To SWITCH.) Just coming.

NICK: *(In the room and on the phone now.)* Yep. OK.

Puts phone down.

LAURA: I'm asleep.

NICK: Oh? You won't want to listen to this then.

LAURA: Who?

NICK: Rupert.

She sits up next to him and hears on the ordinary landline. We hear the conversation with TONY is already underway.

RUPERT: Well I just wanted you to know that I've been speaking today to Rumsfeld.

TONY: Right.

RUPERT: No doubt he's dead set on going ahead. Not going to let this opportunity slip away, he says. Won't get another chance.

TONY: Right.

RUPERT: Don's boys need Diego Garcia, Tony.

TONY: Well Rupert I am aware of that. I've been in discussion with them on that.

RUPERT: Needs the British base there. He'll go without it, Tony, make no mistake, but he'd like to have it. So it's your call. We'll be with you.

TONY: Right. Thanks Rupert.

Pause of a few seconds. Hear breathing.

RUPERT: It's the right decision, Tony. Believe me.

Phone cuts off.

NICK looks at LAURA who appears stunned. Puts the phone down. NICK starts putting it back in its box.

Long pause.

LAURA struggling not to explode.

LAURA: So.

Pause. Silence.

So that's it then. That's what we've been waiting for.

Pause. Pacing about. Looking at NICK who is avoiding her stare.

It's Rupert who decides. Right?

NICK leaves the room.

(To herself.) I wish I hadn't heard that call. Why did you let me hear that call? I really didn't want to hear that one. Now what?

Emotional. Thrashes out.

NICK comes back in.

LAURA: I feel sick.
This nobody would ever believe. And certainly nobody would print it. Not now.
And because nobody would believe it – or print it – you can do it.

NICK: So you want us to let the Americans down. And miss the only chance we'll ever have to get rid of him?

LAURA: I want you to be true to yourself Nick. True to what you believe.

Doorbell rings.

NICK: And what might that be?

LAURA shrieks and thrashes out again. Picks up a pillow and throws it across the room.

Holds his shoulders and looks into his eyes.

LAURA: Are you in there? I see only dead eyes, you've been brainwashed.

Silence. He pulls away from her.

NICK: So you want your friend Saddam to stay in power do you?

LAURA: That's really Stalinist.

NICK: Stalin or Hitler, you and Marisia should make your minds up.

LAURA: You've brought – poison right into our house. With your war. You know that. And it's infecting everything.

NICK: When in five years' time we have a democratic Iraq and peace in Palestine you'll apologise I hope.

LAURA: Oh God. What's going to happen? What?

She bangs the wall and a vast piece of plaster comes crashing down.

Sound of crying children.

What is going to happen?

MARISIA's steps heard.

NICK: *(Reciting, hyped up/manic/robotic, pacing the room.)* Special forces cross and seal borders within 24 hours; hit Baghdad with overwhelming force; capture Saddam; find and neutralise all WMD; disarm the army and bring in peace-keepers. Monitor refugee flows. Restore order and calm.

LAURA: No. *(Loud.)* Nick. Listen. I mean. What's going to happen to us?

Landline rings.

NICK: Hi. *(To TONY.)* Yes, of course.

LAURA: Nick! Nick! Nick!

NICK: Sure. *(False laugh.)*
Just bear with me one minute could you…

(To LAURA.) You're frightening the children and I can't hear. This is important Laura. Could you just… *(Points at the door.)*

LAURA: OK yes I will go and I won't come back.

NICK: *(To TONY.)* Rumsfeld's clearly in control now.

Pacing.

LAURA: Yes he obviously is! And no actually – you leave. And take that man with you. *(Snatches phone out of his hand and throws it out of the door.)* And these. *(Picks up red boxes and throws them out.)* Out of my bedroom. Get out. Both of you. *(Hits out at him. He falls back against the step ladder which falls on him as he leaves the door. Big crash outside. And a muffled cry from NICK.)*

SCENE FIVE

A few days later. Stockwell bedroom.

Middle of the night. Bedroom is dark but we are aware of step ladder still fallen down and chaos of the fight earlier. NICK is asleep in bed. LAURA comes in carefully. Has obviously been out late. Takes down hair. Goes to bathroom. Comes back in pyjamas. Seems a bit wobbly. Closes door so room nearly black. Gets into bed trying not to wake NICK. After a few moments the landline rings on NICK's side of the bed. He wakes up like a shot and answers it.

NICK: OK. Yes it's Nick Beeching here. Yes. *(Sits bolt upright in the bed. Still in total darkness.)* I see. Yes. Of course. Yes I'll make sure he's told. Thank you Colonel.

LAURA sits up and turns around.

LAURA: *(Frightened. Seeing NICK's in shock, staring ahead.)* What is it? What is it?

NICK: *(Head in hands. We see his arm is in a sling.)* It's started.

LAURA: And?

NICK: British helicopter down. Twelve Marines dead.

LAURA: *(Sobbing.)* Oh God no. Oh no.

> *NICK gets up and paces around a little. Then goes to the phone and dials the Number 10 Switchboard. Coughs. Can't speak at first... controls himself.*

NICK: It's Nick. Can I have the Duty Clerk.

Tom, hi. We need to wake the Prime Minister. Yes. I'm coming in.

(To LAURA.) I'll have to be with him.

> *He has an arm in a sling and is struggling into clothes with one arm. Goes to bathroom. A little light comes in now. NICK comes out of bathroom dressed and leaves the room. Goes downstairs. As he does a beep of an alarm about to go off starts up.*

NICK: *(Shouts up from below.)* Where's the code for Mervin's new alarm? Laura, Laura. Bloody hell. Laura! Where is it? Quick.

> *LAURA in darkness fumbles for a drawer, steps out and falls over the stepladder. Obviously panicking now lying flat out on the floor.*

NICK: Quick. It's going to go off any minute.

> *Beeping continues getting louder. Then NICK appears at the open door. Beeping getting louder. He is looking down at her. She shrieks and struggles to get up. Sense of panic as a light is knocked to the floor and suddenly the screeching alarm goes off.*

SCENE SIX

The Stockwell bedroom. September 2003.

LAURA: *(Narrating.)* The months immediately after the start of war are still blurred in my mind – which is probably just as well. Conversations that I never thought I'd have, started turning over in my head. *(Picks up a child's toy.)*

By the summer we were down in Devon where at least the calls couldn't reach us on the beach. But up the long path from the cove the signal would come and go and often he'd drop the buckets and spades and slump on the bank, listening to the horrors. The children would sit down next to him, hold his hand, and wait.

The worst news seemed to come when we reached the top of the hill where the sun breaks through by the church. There we heard about Sergio, the UN envoy. He was blown up in one of the first suicide bombs. And then I got a text about Mazen, my friend the Palestinian cameraman, from Hebron. He'd been posted to Baghdad for Reuters and was shot dead while filming, by American soldiers.

Then the inquiries were suddenly upon us so we were back in London, trying to carry on as normal. It wasn't easy.

One Saturday a green Rover pulled up at the door in Stockwell and there was Tom with the biggest pile of red boxes I had ever seen. Inside was every email sent by Number Ten about the Iraq war.

TOM: *(Enters kitchen carrying in piles of boxes.)* Is he about?

LAURA: He's out at the climbing wall with the children.

TOM: Well this is his weekend homework. Got to read it by Monday.
In here OK?

LAURA: Yeah fine.

LAURA moves washing off table.

TOM: Vauxhall Bridge was closed this morning. Had to come over Chelsea Bridge and back down the South Circular.

LAURA: The South Circular!

TOM: So I'd better be getting back. Just sign for it could you please Laura. *(He leaves, passing MARISIA who is coming into the kitchen.)* Hello Marisia, alright?

MARISIA: Oh hello Tom. Working Saturdays now?

TOM: 24/7.

LAURA now busily looks through the boxes pulling papers out and looking at them.

LAURA: Where are Nick's? *(Keeps looking.)*

MARISIA: *(Starts poking in another box.)* Look here…

LAURA: Let me see… Let me see… *(Takes some papers.)* 2002… June, July… September. *(Reading, flicking through, as if hard to believe.)* November… Dossier can only convince the converted… What? GB says… can't afford the war… December …Tony hysterical 'Need smoking gun'. *(Sits down. Takes a pile with her. Reads some more.)* Jan. 'Intelligence does nothing to demonstrate an imminent threat.'

MARISIA: But…?

LAURA: Wait. Look at this… *(As if to herself. Suddenly. Emotional.)* I knew that's what he thought. *(Stands.)* I knew it. Thank God.

MARISIA looks puzzled.

Noise of NICK coming in door. LAURA walks around and around holding another paper. Looking at it.

NICK: Hello I need a hand here.

MARISIA: I'm coming. *(Leaves.)*

LAURA: *(Alone, reading the paper in her hand.)* 'War without second resolution inconceivable'.

Pause, looks towards door.

She puts this note up against a fruit bowl. NICK comes in.

You're back early.

NICK: *(Comes in carrying newspapers, which he puts down on the breakfast bar.)* They got right to the top of the wall today. *(NICK looks towards the boxes, puzzled.)* What's all that?

LAURA: Just a few of your little notes and emails.

NICK: Oh yes, they said they were sending something over. Before my evidence. *(Shrugs. Starts to flick through the newspapers.)*

LAURA: Don't you want to see?

NICK: They both did really well on the wall today, you should have come.

LAURA: Look! It's what you wrote. To him. I knew you must have.

NICK picks up note. Examines it. Affects disinterest.

NICK: Well I may have put a note in his box on that. So?

LAURA: 'Inconceivable!' Nick. Your word not mine. Not just – a bit of a bad idea!

You didn't tell me you were telling him that.

NICK: Look it wasn't like that. You don't understand. As usual.

LAURA: Well what I understand is that I have to find out what you think – thought – like this, searching round in secret boxes, that have been driven round and round the South Circular all morning.

It's like… working in the archives again – trying to understand what people said to each other about… I don't know… Stalingrad or something.

Except in this case I have to hunt in boxes to find out what the man I live with didn't say to me.

And all because you still have to pretend to be on his side.

NICK: Give me a break Laura. Please. It's a weekend.

LAURA: But I'm so… pleased… at least I know what you really thought now… *(Hugs him. Then moves away.)* Though it's a very odd way to communicate with your wife – not that I am your wife, of course.

Pause.

NICK: I need a coffee.

NICK drinks coffee. Then wanders over to the boxes and starts poking in them. Pulls one or two out. Laughs as if surprised.

LAURA: April. 'T depressed… about chaos of the aftermath.' May. 'George sends card to wish T happy birthday.'

NICK: Look, I'd forgotten we did that. 'A list of party rules for a PM's resignation mid-parliament'. Cabinet Secretary dug them out just before the vote. God we must have been worried.
And here's the one you found under the bed – that he wrote to George. 'You can count on me whatever.'

LAURA: That's your edited version!

NICK: *(Stuff emails back in box and pulls a map out of his back pocket.)* By the way I thought we might go trekking in the Dolomites next year. I've planned it all out for you to look at – here. The children could manage that too I think. Could even be a sort of honeymoon – what do you think? Staying in mountain huts.∴?

LAURA: Inconceivable.

She's still looking through the emails. Ignores the comment.

NICK: What's for lunch? I'm starving?
I'll put some spaghetti on then.

He starts chopping carrots and putting a saucepan on.

He has this word for it actually. Carapace. Those closest, he says, have to be inside a carapace. Then we can all say what we think, without it getting out.

Looks up.

LAURA: Carapace?

Pulls out a dictionary.

Carapace. Carapace… consists of large, rigid plates of armaplas fitted to parts of body. It's stronger and thicker than normal flak armour. Its notable disadvantage is it can be tiring to wear in extended battles. *(Looks at NICK.)* No wonder you couldn't see what was going on.
Do you still all crawl inside this carapace thing? Even now?

Pause.

Doesn't it occur to you that I need to know what the closest person to me thinks about it too?

NICK: Oh stop it now. I've had enough. I'm going for a bath.

LAURA: Just trying to find out what you think.

NICK: To look at it your way as always.

LAURA: You're looking at it his way – still. You know what *(Laughs.)* – Martha asked me the other day, whether it was like – suddenly waking up one day and realising you'd married Mrs Thatcher?

NICK: What?

LAURA: That's what I said.

NICK: Well if they think I'm going to read all that by Monday they're wrong. There isn't time.

LAURA: I'll read them for you then. I'll enjoy that.
Maybe I'll find Tony's answers to you. So we'll know what he thinks too – now that would be –

NICK: Unlikely. He hardly wrote anything down.
You know he asked me once why I wrote those notes. Said

I did it purely for the historical record. *(As if to himself.)*
That really irritated me.

NICK: Anyhow, you can read into those whatever you want.
(Points at the boxes.) If it helps.
Put the spaghetti on. I'm going for a bath.

LAURA: I will. And it does.

NICK: *(He starts to leave the room then pauses to point at something in the newspaper on the breakfast bar.)* And remember, they're still searching for those WMD. There's a story here saying the weapons inspectors may have found some biological stuff buried in the desert out near Babylon. It's by Jim Johnson.

He looks at her then leaves the room.

LAURA: *(Shouting after him.)* You should take your armour off, then you'll see better.

LAURA: *(Alone narrating.)* After that we had a truce. Those notes were like – peace offerings for me. We were on the same planet after all. That's how I saw it anyhow. OK, yes, how I wanted to see it. And at least for a while we were able to stop arguing about the war. Pensions was their new topic, as if Iraq hadn't happened.
But I always knew the truce wouldn't hold.

Act Two

SCENE ONE

The Stockwell bedroom September 2004.

LAURA and NICK are asleep in bed. A radio alarm goes off and the Today programme starts. It is 6.30am. A child starts shouting from offstage. A tricycle lies on its side by the door.

NICK gets up and goes out to take a shower. We hear the shower start up.

The phone by the bed goes. She turns over and looks at the clock. Ignores it. It stops ringing after four rings. She opens her eyes, suggesting she knows something we don't.

A mobile phone on the chest of drawers then immediately starts ringing in a different ringtone. That also stops after precisely four rings. A Blackberry next to the mobile then immediately and insistently starts buzzing and jumping around.

The sound of the Today programme continues in the background.

RADIO NEWS ANNOUNCER: Eighteen months after the start of the war in Iraq, investigators in Iraq are understood to have completed their inquiries into Saddam Hussein's weapons of mass destruction, and will announce that no significant traces of WMD have been found. If confirmed, the news will cause alarm in Washington and London where government sources continue to insist that Saddam's WMD were a justification for going to war.

According to leaks of the ISG report, the comprehensive 15-month search for weapons of mass destruction in Iraq has concluded that the only chemical or biological agents that Saddam Hussein's regime possessed were small quantities of poisons, most likely for use in assassinations.

The report is also believed to conclude that that there was evidence to suggest the Iraqi regime planned to restart its illegal weapons programmes if UN sanctions were lifted.

LAURA sits up and shouts from the bedroom to the bathroom.

LAURA: It's Switch.

The Blackberry falls silent.

NICK: *(Shouting from under the shower.)* Tell them to wait.

LAURA: Tell them yourself.

ED: *(The Today programme presenter on radio.)* So Foreign Secretary this was an illegal war wasn't it? We now know there was no threat to this country. And now we're hearing that the Iraq Survey Group is going to say there were no weapons of mass destruction. All stockpiles had been destroyed after the first Gulf War…

JACK: Look Ed. Let's wait for the Iraq Survey Group to report. It would be premature to anticipate the ISG findings but we are confident that there was every reason to suppose at that juncture that Saddam had at least the intent and the potential capacity to put into operation within a period of time which could have been a period threatening to us not only in relation to CW but also BW as well. And don't forget, Ed, as many people have, and do, that tests on SPMCs, though at a very early stage of development, had shown – indeed proven – that if combined in a missile, could have had a range of up to 2000 kilometres with a 500k payload which would…

LAURA sits up. Looks at clock again. Doorbell rings again. She gets out of bed and picks up an intercom phone on the wall. Looks at it.

LAURA: Decorators. Who told them to start this early?

ED: You've seen the ISG draft have you?

NICK re-enters in towel and switches off the radio.

NICK: Course he hasn't seen a draft.

Phones start ringing in turn again. First the landline, four times, then the mobile jingle four times. NICK is just about to pick it up when it stops. He holds his hand over the Blackberry and catches it on first ring.

NICK: Hi. *(To TONY in his relaxed Downing Street-I'm-speaking-to-TONY kind of 'Hi'.)*

I'm in my bedroom.
No, not exactly.

He looks at LAURA and the intercom.

Because I was in the shower, if you must know. Now I'm in the bedroom. Getting dressed.
No. I have not yet had breakfast. Yes. I have seen the ISG draft report. I'm the one who put it in your box last night, as you know. With a note.
I agree it doesn't look good. But did you read my line-to-take note?

Walks back to the bathroom looking at LAURA holding the towel and the phone. Then he stops, suddenly, on the way.

No. Look. One thing at a time. We mustn't panic. OK so it's bad. The headlines will be appalling. But it depends a bit how you read it. I mean some of it's actually quite helpful to us.
Of finding them now? Err no.
No it isn't.

(Raising his voice a little.) We have got some time. It's not being published for at least two weeks. We have a firm agreement with Washington on that. Let's look and see what we can salvage from it.

Then into the bathroom and out again.

Stops in his tracks again.

No you are not going to have to resign.

Stuffs a tie in his pocket. Pulls on trainers. Stuffs another tie in the other pocket and pulls one out that's already in there.

Look, let's – keep calm. No it isn't. There's a paragraph about SPMCs we can use.

Solid Propellant Motor Cases.

Yes but the fact is that we weren't the only ones to believe the intelligence.

LAURA looks towards NICK suddenly.

What we have to remember and make sure everyone is aware of is that the whole world believed it. CIA, MOSSAD, BND, DGSE – yes, even the French. Everyone knew he had them. At that time they all knew it. It was clear.

Ok. Not true, perhaps. But clear. Certainly. That has to be the line to get out.

LAURA now shaking her head.

Well, it may be the only line we have. And it's a good one. They all believed it. And let's not forget that Parliament believed it too. Because they all believed you. Believe me.

LAURA is now standing in pyjamas by his side trying to hear. He waves her away and puts a finger on one ear.

You know how these things are. Just hold on. Chances are it won't be that big a story on the day. Put up a safe pair of hands. We've still got strategic intent to fall back on. You'll see that in the briefing paper.

I don't know. God no. He's going in the reshuffle isn't he?

Listens, signalling to LAURA, pointing to the wardrobe. He needs a shirt. She pulls a neatly ironed one off a hanger and he screws it up and stuffs it in a rucksack with his spare hand, still balancing the phone. He signals to LAURA to bring over a red box. She heaves it over and he takes out a massive pile of documents and stuffs them into his rucksack on top of his shirt. 'Mummy, Mummy,' is heard from outside and a loud bang.

LAURA: Wait I'm coming.

She goes out. Heard shouting outside the door.

Marisia? Are you there? Please? Marisia?

NICK goes into the bathroom, phone still at his ear.

NICK: Sorry. I didn't hear that.

LAURA comes back into the room and MARISIA appears at the door in pyjamas holding a teddy bear and a sandwich box. Gives the box to LAURA who stuffs it in the rucksack.

MARISIA: Wow. Calls are starting early. It's like the war all over again.

NICK comes back in.

NICK: Yes you can. Yes good. I'm glad you read that too.

LAURA picks up a pair of scruffy shoes, looks at them and stuffs them in the rucksack.

NICK: Yes, good. I'm glad you read that too.
(Sits down.) Now that might be something to resign about –
err sorry. I meant to worry about.
Yes you're absolutely right. It's much, much more
important than the ISG.
It came in late last night from Berlin and we have to
discuss it before this dinner.
You know what dinner.
C's dinner you remember?
You agreed to have a small dinner in the flat for him – for
his retirement.
Yes you do know about it.
It's been in the diary for ages. You agreed it was a good
move.

Pause.

Decorator comes into the room carrying a ladder and goes into the bathroom. NICK ignores him.

Look there's a conference call with Berlin this morning.
Let's fix a meeting for after that. With Alastair and
Graham. But we can discuss this when I get in.
Twenty minutes.
On my bike. How do you think I get around for God's
sake? I don't have outriders unlike some people.

NICK: Yes I can do it in 20 minutes.
I live in a place called Stockwell, as you know. It's
somewhere south of the river in a part of London you
never venture to. Yes I can.

LAURA tries to clip the rucksack on him.

NICK: Over Vauxhall Bridge. No, Westminster's closed. For
the protest? I thought it was for repairs. Look, thanks for
the directions. Very touching. But don't worry about me
and put the coffee on. See you in 20 minutes.

*Puts the phone down. Finishes dressing. Puts on an anorak and
starts pulling on trainers.*

Sandwiches?

LAURA signals they are in the rucksack.

LAURA: Is it true that he's still got no idea where Stockwell is?

NICK says nothing.

LAURA: Course he knows. Ridiculous.
But God! So he's really going to resign is he? Did he say
that?

She looks at NICK for a reaction. NICK still says nothing.

No? But they found nothing at all did they?

NICK: Not a lot.

LAURA: Nothing – absolutely not a scintilla of a weapon of
mass destruction. There's nothing you can spin. *(Picks up
large document and flicks through it.)* Well, maybe you can use

some of this stuff on page 99 – they found a few botulism
seeds. But otherwise you've only got intent to fall back on.

NICK: *(Half teasing.)* You've started reading my bloody papers
again.

LAURA: You've started leaving them lying around again.

NICK: What's on page 99 again? *(He starts flicking through the
ISG draft report.)*

He's just panicking. He won't resign.

Looks up.

LAURA: But he might have to go. I mean – at least it's clear
now that this isn't just about lying. It's about catastrophic
error. I mean getting it totally and utterly 100 per cent
wrong.

NICK: Don't… start…

LAURA: Are you more likely to have to resign for lying or for
getting something totally wrong?

NICK: Lying obviously.

LAURA: Getting it wrong's just as bad – or in his case, just not
looking for the truth. A kind of lying to yourself in fact.

All those duff sources. Imagine the questions now.

Pause.

LAURA: But what do you think. Might he throw in the towel
after all?

NICK: No. I mean… not over this. *(He sounds just ever-so-slightly
uncertain for a moment.)*

LAURA: Over what then? There's something else going on isn't
there? *(To herself.)* Oh God. Now what? What is it?

NICK: Nothing.

LAURA: What was the talk of Berlin? Something from Berlin.

She walks to the window and seems to be trying to recollect something. Looks agitated. Then she goes to a box, searches, and pulls out a pile of notebooks. Searches them.

I remember now. Here it is. 'German source has new intelligence that clinches it – George.' Seems to be… what? Can't read my shorthand. What's the date here? March 4th 2003.

NICK: Here let me look at that. What was the date of that? *(Takes notebook from her.)*

LAURA: That's it isn't it. Something about a German source. Good job someone kept a record of that then wasn't it? Daisy. I've written. So Daisy was important right?

He rips the page out of her notebook.

Hey, get off. It's mine.

NICK: You'll get it back. I thought it was much earlier. As late as that was it? Jesus.

The child cries again and she rushes out. NICK struggling with rucksack while she's out. She comes back a moment later.

NICK: Here help me could you?

NICK heaves rucksack onto his back.

Pause.

LAURA: So do you think he might have to go then. I mean over this Daisy thing?

NICK: *(Looking at the decorator.)* Are they ever going to finish?

LAURA: It's all going to blow up again isn't it. I can feel it. What would make him resign? Not being hoaxed by Saddam – obviously. So what? Something worse. Oh God. You know I think I'd better come after all. Tonight. To the dinner.

NICK: Can't keep away then? You said you wouldn't go to these dinners again. Never ever again you said.

LAURA: I know I did. And I meant it. But I think I should tonight. Spouses are invited aren't they?

NICK: Are you sure it's a good idea?

LAURA: Who's coming again?

NICK: Just C – and friends.

LAURA: But maybe I shouldn't go.

(To NICK.) What do you think?

NICK: What? Yes come if you want – he's always asking why you don't come any more.

LAURA: Really? He is?

NICK: Can't think why.

LAURA: Well maybe I'll come then. It has to be interesting. Whatever they say. Doesn't it?

NICK: I wouldn't count on it. *(Looking at her.)* But you won't – will you?

LAURA: What?

NICK grabs his Number Ten pass.

NICK: And you'll need to get Marisia to babysit. We've got the school play too – maybe I can squeeze that in on the way to the airport.

LAURA: And you've got Go Ape on Saturday morning don't forget.
Worse than lying and worse than getting the reason for going to war completely and utterly wrong. Jesus. So he really might resign.

NICK: I don't know. Not today anyhow. No time. We've got a reshuffle on.
I'll clear you in the gate for 6.45. You'd better be on time. Security will be really tight for this one. How on earth we're going get through this bloody reshuffle in one day I don't know. I've really got to go.

He goes out the door then comes back.

Got any ideas for new Foreign Secretary?

LAURA: Ummm… What about Margaret?

NICK: Margaret?

LAURA: Why not? Stands her ground well. Not Jack.

NICK: Yeah. Maybe. I'll try her on him.

LAURA's mobile phone goes.

LAURA: I'll ring you back.

NICK: So don't be late for the dinner tonight.

LAURA: Helmet. What did you think of the paint?

NICK: *(He shouts out of the door.)* Marisia can you babysit tonight?

MARISIA: I'm supposed to be out with the girls… but…

NICK: Well don't let me stop you…

MARISIA: No it's OK. Yes OK.

NICK: Well thanks. I'm off.

The door slams downstairs loudly.

Peace descends. LAURA seems marooned amongst bedclothes and strewn papers. Makes notes in her notebook. Picks up clothing. Makes the bed. Opens wardrobe containing small TV and switches it on.

TV NEWS REPORTER: Several ministers face the axe today as the Prime Minister prepares a major reshuffle…

LAURA watches for a while. Stops. Starts flicking through a notebook. Then picks up another and starts making notes.

Her mobile goes again.

LAURA: Hi Jim. *(Looks at watch.)* Deadlines are early nowadays.
The ISG report? No I haven't heard anything about that at

all. Who's telling you?
No of course I haven't seen it. *(Picks report up, flicks through it.)* No I am not. No.

Puts report down and picks up her notebook. Flicks back through it. Reads carefully.

Underlines something. Puts notebook in bag.

SCENE TWO

Number Ten Downing Street. Evening of the same day. September 2004.

TONY's bedroom.

TONY is sitting on a bed, which is covered with a thick quilted bedspread. The room is dominated by a cumbersome running machine. A wardrobe runs the full length of one wall. A toy tricycle lies on its side. A bowl of apples sits on a table.

NICK is peering through the rear window. He looks different as he's wearing a very expensive-looking suit, but one of his shoelaces is undone. And his demeanour is different here. The whole atmosphere is ordered/relaxed.

We are also aware of another room below, which is in a half-light. A man is sitting there staring at a computer screen. He is TOM the Number Ten Duty Clerk. On one wall of the office is a giant TV which is on but mute.

TONY stands up and we see he is in his underpants. He is on the phone. TONY glances at himself in the large dressing table mirror often.

TONY: Yes… but you see…
Yeah. But I'm trying to explain that…
Well, OK, sure… but we can't have the Chief of Defence Staff resigning…

He then pulls on trousers and points to the wardrobe signalling to NICK that he needs a shirt. NICK opens the wardrobe – revealing an endless line of shirts – and pulls one out. TONY checks the collar and rejects it. Asks for another one. Still on the phone. Signalling now he wants help with the cufflinks. Looks at himself in the mirror again and signals to NICK to get out of his line of vision.

Of course I understand you have your problems but believe me I have a few of my own as a matter of fact. Yeah. OK Gordon. Well look we can work this thing out. But I have to run now I've got a dinner but let's touch base later.

He puts the phone down and stands right up to the mirror, examining his appearance quite carefully, especially his hair.

NICK: They've moved them back down to the park now. Heck of a lot of them.

Looks at his notes.

So… Tomorrow – French ambassador's in at 8am then Gordon's at 8.15 then you're at the airport at 10 and…

TONY: *(Interrupting.)* He went bloody ballistic about Margaret moving to the Foreign Office.

NICK: Ha. *(As if well there's a surprise!)* She was gob-smacked apparently.
And… at 12 you have a call with Paisley but I've just realised we'll be in the air so… then Rupert's in for a drink at 6 – again.

TONY moves his arm in a sliced backhand volley action. Then gets out his shoes and brushes them assiduously. Now looking at NICK's shoes.

TONY: You really need to get yourself some new shoes Nick. I mean look at them. I'll take you to Churches tomorrow.

NICK examines his shoes.

TONY: And your socks are – revolting. Is that paint or something?

NICK: Marisia put something blue in the wash.

TONY: The Bialystock plumber? We had a Pole once… quite a…

A child's voice is heard outside the door. A crash. NICK rushes out to investigate. Comes back.

NICK: I've put him in the playpen. Errr. So you have to get some words from Paisley on the OTRs.

TONY: Look, just… you know… I mean… before tomorrow we have to get through this dinner tonight. Whose bloody idea was it anyway? On a day like this? I mean we have the Iraq Survey Group about to declare an intelligence fiasco on Iraq just as I am entertaining C and his mates to dinner. Doesn't look great does it?

NICK gives up on the agenda and reaches for an apple from the bowl. TONY snatches the bowl away from him.

TONY: They're mine.

NICK: *(Disappointed about the apple.)* Nobody's going to know about it. One of those dinners that didn't happen.

TONY: Yeah, like the WMD that didn't happen?

NICK: You sound like my wife.

TONY: Thought you two weren't married. *(Looks around a moment.)* Why not, as a matter of interest? Weren't you going to get married a while back…

NICK doesn't respond.

TONY: Beth said Laura really hates me now… she doesn't does she…?

NICK: Look…

TONY: I always thought we got on OK. She coming tonight?

NICK: Maybe… look can we… stick to the point. And you have to take this chance to ask C about this Daisy business.

TONY: Daisy… *(NICK looks intently at him.)*

He stops polishing his shoes and looks up at NICK.

Yeah. I got that same look from Alastair this afternoon. Alastair, I mean what's going on there. Got a match tonight… says Spiegel is running an exclusive about it this weekend. Can't have been our best source can he?

Looks at NICK who shrugs.

So tell me what we know. Or what did we know? I'm not sure I quite remember where this Daisy character even fitted in. Do you? I mean where do they get these code names from for God's sake. Daisy. I ask you!
And why on earth does this one guy matter so much? Surely we had lots of sources?

NICK: But Daisy is – was – the only half credible source we have left on WMD. And he's about to be blown wide open. Looks like he might have been a total fraud.

TONY: Right. But – so – how?

NICK: OK so the Germans get hold of him somehow just before the UN vote. Their intelligence guys apparently signal that their new asset – Daisy – has great new stuff on mobile BW which the Americans jump at saying it clinches the whole WMD story. Much better than any of that rubbish on 45 minutes. George mentioned Daisy in a call to you – very excited.

TONY: Right… when exactly was that? Is there a note of it?

NICK: As you know, you wouldn't have note-takers on those calls… so… but I happen to have a note here.

NICK gets the note he tore from LAURA's notebook. Reads it out. It has a few of her comments he wasn't expecting.

NICK: Here… March 4th 2003. 9.00pm. George. Germans have new Iraqi source. Shows C has them.

He hands TONY the note.

TONY: *(Reading.)* 'Sonofabitch… will offload… Jesus'. What?

NICK: Sorry, err, anyhow, so that was when it was. A few days before we went in. Then it turned out C had mentioned it to you in a meeting the same day. One of those cosy meetings I wasn't in on... you may remember. So... no record of that at all.

TONY: *(Looks at him.)* Right. Pass me that comb.

But if the ISG say there were no weapons of mass destruction why does it matter that Daisy turns out half-baked too. Adds up to the same almighty cock-up doesn't it?

NICK: Yeah. But the ISG says we were wrong but honestly wrong. And as long as we get our line out early and make sure we project the bits where we weren't totally and utterly wrong it'll come out OK... you see. And there's some quite useful stuff on page 99 of the ISG draft you might want to look at.
So we've been moving our position to, yes, we were wrong but what is wrong? By weighing in with the backstory we show everyone else was too. And Saddam was a very bad man etc, etc. So we say we were – right to be wrong – in a way.

TONY: *(Unconvinced.)* Yeah.

NICK: But the next thing they'll want to know is who gave us this duff information. Who our source was? The point about Daisy is that nobody is going to understand how we could possibly have believed this guy. Our German contacts suggest his story is so unbelievably gobsmacking that nobody will accept we ever took it seriously. The press'll just say it just proves we never had any evidence and must have been lying about WMD. That Daisy was part of a conspiracy.

TONY: Ummm. Which is worse – I mean in the public's mind – lying or getting it just – very wrong?

NICK: I don't know. Laura thinks it makes no difference...

TONY: Umm...

NICK: But look – it may not be so bad. Daisy may turn out to be more believable than we fear.

TONY: OK… go on.

NICK: On the other hand he may not. *(TONY looks at him, confused.)*

TONY: Well what was he – she – I mean, this asset… it did exist then?

NICK: As far as we can tell, yes. Some sort of conman. But there is no paper trail on this over here at all. I'm checking all the traffic this morning, but so far not a trace. And it's worse than that. When we spoke this morning, Berlin insisted they had warned Washington off him. *(Pause.)* So the only mention we have of Daisy is in this note.

Waves LAURA's scrappy note.

TONY: What is that? *(TONY reaches out for it. NICK keeps it back.)* Get rid of it whatever it is.

NICK: *(Putting note back in his pocket.)* So anything you can remember of what C might have said to you – in private – would be useful.

TONY: There was something. C seemed very excited by a German source at one point. Would deliver, he said. That's all I can remember.
And you know… C's talk was all about assets and sub-sources and stuff. I mean. I don't know. You know that language they talk. It sounded – pretty confusing but pretty convincing. And he'd just come in and say this or that asset knew Saddam had the stuff – hidden in a palace or under a school or some such thing then when Blix's people didn't find it, his line was that they'd just spirited it all away somewhere. That kind of thing. He promised me he'd find them in time. I remember that. He said he knew where they were.

NICK: So we need to know tonight from C exactly who Daisy was, what he said, what we did with what he said, how much we relied on him, and why.

TONY: Right. Shouldn't someone have asked that at the time?

NICK: Err – yes. Perhaps you should.

TONY: Fuck off Nick. Your sense of humour, it's…

NICK: Well, sorry, but you did have these tête-à-têtes with C…

Knock. TOM, the Duty Clerk enters.

TONY: Hi Tom.

TOM: To sign. *(Gives NICK some papers for the PM to sign.)*

TONY: You Duty Clerk tonight Tom?

TOM: I am, Prime Minister.

TONY: Anything about?

TOM: Signal that Washington may want a call. They'll revert. Chancellor's been on. A few times. And… here's the guest list. *(Gives it to NICK.)*

NICK: Thanks Tom.

TONY: OK. So, who's coming?

TOM: Oh, and security are warning not go on the terrace tonight. The protest.

NICK: Your American friend James is C's guest of honour.

TONY: Have I seen James since George kicked him out?

NICK: Last saw him at Camp David – you fancied his wife.

TONY: *(Raising an eyebrow.)* Did I? Don't remember. Name? *(NICK looks at the list.)* Abigail. And I think you saw him in the margins at the Azores…

TONY: What's he doing now?

NICK: Don't know. Nothing. Been slagging off the administration quite a bit. Revealing all in his memoirs maybe…

TONY: What?

TONY looks round, horrified.

NICK: No, just kidding.

NICK hands TONY the piece of paper.

Here are the others. We've kept it small. *(TONY reads down and moves to a writing desk with a pen in a stand and some paper. He takes out the fountain pen and sits poised to make a note.)*

TONY: So what am I going to say about C tonight? Give me some words. I mean 'Thanks for everything you've done' – doesn't sound quite right does it?

NICK: Well, let's see, err – Cold War was his heyday. Rumour that he smuggled Gordievsky out of Moscow in a boot of a car – or was that Bob? Likes to throw his weight about – they say.

TONY: Jesus. Those guys. I mean, you know them Nick. What makes them tick? And why the hell have we got this dinner at all? We don't usually entertain these people do we?

He puts down the pen. Puts on a jacket then takes it off and sticks with the shirtsleeve look.

NICK: No. But you two had this – special friendship. And Graham thought it would be a good move – keep The Service on our side – especially now. You'll think of something. Just make it up. You always do.

TONY registers the jibe.

TONY: The Service! *(Thinks. Pause.)*

NICK: But really, you're good at that kind of thing. Off the cuff. Those ministers you sacked today didn't realise they were sacked until they were out of the door.

TONY looks at NICK.

Just flatter him a little.

TONY: Can you flatter a spy?

NICK: This one, sure.

SCENE THREE

Number Ten. Early evening of the same day.

The Outer Office.

The Outer Office is the nerve centre of Number Ten. It has two doors leading off – one to the PM's office and one to the corridor and the front door. As action takes place in the Outer Office we are also aware of things going on in a connected sitting room – and vice versa. Beyond is a dining room.

As the scene opens in the Outer Office there is a sound of faint chanting of a crowd, but all noise is cushioned.

At one desk sits the duty clerk, TOM, who is typing into his computer. He also takes brief calls, often, and talks almost inaudibly on the telephone. It is as if he likes not to be noticed.

At the other desk – which is NICK's – is a large empty swivel chair. On one wall are three large clocks showing the time in Moscow, Washington and London. Taking up almost the whole of another wall is a vast TV screen showing Sky News but the volume is still off.

Then LAURA comes through the Number Ten front door, looking for NICK to go with him to the dinner. We see her wander down the corridor to the outer office. We are also aware of NICK still being in the bedroom with TONY as she enters.

TOM: Hello Laura. How's things?

LAURA: Oh fine thanks Tom. Am I late?

TOM: Just mingling, I think you'd call it. Your other half is in the bedroom with the boss.

He just called down to say would you go on in without him. Something's come up.

LAURA: Oh right. I think I'll wait here for him though.

Have you seen this Tom? Nick's dad beside his spitfire.

TOM: Yeah. Got a DFO didn't he? Don't make them like that anymore Laura.

Switchboard rings.

LAURA: *(Narrating.)* Maybe I can't... keep away. From his home – the other man's home.

I mean you walk in past all those tourists at the gate and at first they think you're one of them but then they see you're not and the policeman says... 'Hello there... alright?'...

Then through security and you're suddenly standing in Downing Street – a figure on an empty set – and as you lift your hand to the knocker the door opens as if by magic. 'Hello there. Alright?' They're all expecting you. 'Know your way down there don't you?'

And there's no question that you might not be one of them, because you're in there. We even share his friends you know – Paddy, Cliff and co – all send us Christmas cards, and we got one last year from Greg – he's chairman of British Nuclear Fuels. Tony and Cherie always send us two.

And here's Graham standing by the Rodin raising his mug of tea to me, and Beth in black trousers gives a smile and then comes Switch – 'Hello there Laura' – and then here, in the outer office, is Tom, running things as always *(Smiles at TOM.)* and *(Looks around.)* on a desk, are photographs of *(Picks them up.)* me and the children.

Puts photos down. Picks another one up. Smiles.

Little sound of a protest outside.

Big protest on tonight Tom.

TOM: Expecting trouble here later. This report's brought them all out again.

LAURA: We've got a couple outside our door in Turret Lane. I even had to tell Marisia to double lock the door.
And by the way who was that man raging at those nice special branch guys at your gate just now?

TOM: Oh that would be C. Arrived without his pass and they wouldn't let him in for the dinner.
Caught him on the CCTV – that's him shouting at the guys.

He shows her a CCTV film on his screen.

LAURA: Oh. *(Turning to TOM.)* Does the PM often have C over for dinner Tom?

TOM: Never before on my watch.

LAURA: And you go back a long way.

TOM: John Major. *(Laughs.)*

LAURA: *(Wandering round the office, looking up at the pictures of Prime Ministers.)* Must be strange working for such different Prime Ministers Tom.

TOM: They're all HMG to me Laura.

LAURA: What was Major like to work for?

TOM: Oh lovely man. Understood the clerical grades. Looked after us duty clerks very well. Major.

LAURA: *(Picks up a photograph on TOM's desk.)* This your Dad, Tom?

TOM: Yes. *(Affectionate chuckle.)*

LAURA goes back over to NICK's desk, which is also piled high with papers and his jacket is on the back of the chair. The bike helmet and the rucksack she strapped on to him that morning are hanging behind on a peg.

She sits in his chair and makes herself at home, swivels round and round on the chair, and watches the silent TV screen. Rearranges photographs. Gets up and rummages in rucksack. Finds a half-eaten packet of biscuits and eats one. Look at her watch. Her phone goes. She eventually finds it in her bag. Sends a message. Switches it off, looking at TOM.

LAURA: Sorry Tom. It's off. I'll leave it here.

The TV suddenly catches her attention.

TV NEWSREADER: One of the biggest surprises in today's cabinet reshuffle was the decision to appoint Margaret Beckett as Foreign Secretary. The new Foreign Secretary said she was honoured to have been asked to take the job, and had not expected it.

LAURA looks up, surprised and smiles. Then the story suddenly switches showing a bombing in Iraq.

A suicide bombing on the outskirts of Baghdad today, left more than 25 dead, and scores more injured, including several children. The attack happened in a crowded market near the centre of the city as shoppers formed long queues for food. The blast followed a series of other deadly attacks in recent days which have killed at least 150 people across the country.

Eye-witnesses said the bombers targeted the market in order to cause the maximum terror at the busiest time of the day. The Iraqi President, Jalal Talabani, said that such attacks would not drive a wedge between...

LAURA: God.

She gets up and moves closer to the screen. TOM looks at the screen then gets up and stands next to her. LAURA and TOM are standing very close to the screen, staring...

TOM: You've been out there Nick says.

LAURA: Yes. *(Looks at him. And back at the screen. They both move closer.)*

As the two of them stare at the TV, TONY appears at the doorway behind them. He glances towards NICK's desk – obviously looking for him – then sees the backs of LAURA and TOM and looks up at the screen briefly then at the clocks. Then he leaves, without them noticing him.

LAURA: I'm being stood up again I guess. I'd better go on my own then Tom. You'll let me know if Marisia calls in…

TOM nods, still staring at the screen. He turns the volume up again. We see him staring for a few moments. She leaves.

Blackout.

SCENE FOUR

LAURA enters a small sitting room where the DIRECTOR and C are chatting in the foreground and a few others are talking in the background. There are two sofas either side of a mantelpiece and a coffee table in the middle of the room with a very large red bound document on it. This is the draft ISG report. Speakers glance at it from time to time.

Drinks are on a side table. There are a few photographs scattered around. And the sound of chanting is louder/closer now.

As LAURA enters nobody notices her at first and she seems to be trying to pick up snatches of conversation.

DIRECTOR: Material breach – no doubt of that. Resolution 1441. Blix was…

C: Oh that arrogant fool… of course 20 per cent of the CW was reconfigured after '94.

Sudden roar from the protesters outside the window. Everyone ignores it except LAURA who tries to see where it's coming from.

DIRECTOR: *(Putting an arm out.)* Oh hello you must be Laura, good to meet you… of course you know David, don't you?

Draws C over.

C: Nice to see you again.

DIRECTOR: David's trying to explain the 'bumps' to me – something mysterious he got up to at Cambridge. Were you there too? Seems everybody here was.

LAURA: Yes.

C: Row?

LAURA: No.

C: College?

LAURA: Girton.

C: Good thighs then. For rowing.

DIRECTOR: My wife's read your book, she's fascinated by the war.

C: War?

LAURA: Oh not this one. I'm banned from writing about the present.

DIRECTOR: Churchill's secret service David. Those brave parachutists – dropped into Gestapo hands.

C: Amateurish shambles. *(Goes off to pour himself a drink.)*

LAURA: *(To the DIRECTOR.)* Has intelligence improved since those days do you think?

DIRECTOR: You know what I always say Laura; intelligence is about as useful as the weather forecast – usually unreliable and sometimes plain wrong. But often the only thing we've got to go on. Isn't that right David?

Loud laughter from the DIRECTOR. C snorts. Sudden silence.

TONY: Hi.

All turn simultaneously towards the door where TONY is standing, in crisp blue shirt, smiling broadly. NICK is standing just behind him. TONY pauses a moment to survey the scene and the guests, then strides in, arms outstretched first towards C.

LAURA watches TONY intently. They both watch TONY as he greets guests.

TONY: David – great to see you. Looking well. Sorry I'm late – just, one of those days.
Cherie sends apologies – lecturing in India… James. How are you?

NICK moves from behind TONY to her side.

TONY: Laura.

LAURA: Hello.

Then steps forward. Both arms out. As if to say – let's be friends. And kisses her on both cheeks. All the guests are watching.

TONY: *(Turning to the DIRECTOR.)* So what's up James? Seems ages. A lot has happened I think we could say – in the meantime.

DIRECTOR: Well, Prime Minister, I was just explaining that I have a lot of time on my hands all of a sudden.

TONY: Yes. I heard.

DIRECTOR: I'm spending it on a New Jersey beach.

TONY: Sounds alright. But look… I was so… sorry about how it turned out for you. Why did he have to let you go like that? I mean… *(Looking mystified.)*

DIRECTOR: Sure. I appreciate that Prime Minister. And now the ISG's going to blow us all out of the water. *(Loudly, he has a booming voice.)* Haven't found a damn thing! After all this time.

TONY: Yes – err – so we hear. *(Turning to C.)* What are you hearing on that?

C looks away at a photograph.

DIRECTOR: Rumsfeld doesn't give a damn of course.

TONY: No? *(Looks towards C.)* Well I thought we might have a quiet word about all that after dinner.

(Looks at document.) Just amongst ourselves.

A loudspeaker system starts up beyond the wall.

NICK: They're talking of closing off Westminster.

LAURA: *(Worried.)* They're not! *(To NICK.)* Perhaps I should get back before they do just in case…

TONY: Come – let's eat before we all get holed up here.

DIRECTOR: I'm sure we all brought parachutes.

C: I nearly had to parachute in myself. *(Glowering.)* Wouldn't let me through the gate. Would you believe it!

NICK: *(As they take seats.)* David you've met Laura.

C: Rowed for Girton I believe.

NICK: *(Glancing with raised eyebrows at LAURA.)* Duff intelligence again David… err. *(Seeing C glaring with annoyance.)* Sorry. Just kidding!

TONY stands to speak. Guests fall silent. Noise of outside protests a little louder.

TONY: Well before we eat, I'd like to say a few words to thank David for all he's done. You know – and I've been thinking about this a great deal of late – the intelligence services really are the unsung heroes of these days.

It's not been an easy time.

But as I've said before we're at our best when at our boldest and you, David, are proof of that. You were on the first plane out to ground zero, and if it hadn't been for you, and your people, we wouldn't now be winning the peace in Iraq. And… it's worth considering for a moment that Afghanistan is a country now freed from the Taliban.

C: Damn right it is.

TONY: Even Gadaffi is listening to us today.

Now I know there a lot of people out there *(Looks to the window.)* with different opinions on this thing. But I wonder if those who marched the streets of London ever thought of all those gassed by Saddam. Would our critics now rather Saddam was still in power? I ask them that?

C and DIRECTOR: Hear hear.

TONY: And of course we would have preferred UN backing but, you know, UN intervention came too late and we had to move on – we couldn't just let history repeat itself with another bully endangering world peace.

This ISG report into Saddam's WMD is now upon us and – maybe what they say is right – perhaps it is. But can we really be so sure? I mean Iraq is a big place to hide things in.

C: Those weapons are still out there. Nobody should doubt that.

We see TOM rushing up the stairs to the sitting room with a message. He waits on the edge of the room till the speech finishes.

TONY: David, there will always be many others who will seek the honour and the glory for all of this, while your service remains in the shadows, as it must. What you do must remain secret. That is the nature of the business you are in. But you know, I, for one have come to understand the tremendous value of your contribution.

And one day we will not only have a democratic Iraq, stability in Afghanistan but also peace between Israel and Palestine. Yes. That too. As long as we have faith.

Pause. Looks around the table.

So let us raise a glass to our unsung heroes.

GUESTS: Unsung heroes. Hear Hear.

Sounds of protests.

LAURA: *(Narrating.)* Faith. It had always bothered me when he used that word – ever since that Saturday in Hyde Park.

We'd been out for a family picnic and when we piled back in the car – parked opposite the Albert Hall – the bomb alarm went off so of course we all jumped out again, except Nick, that is. He was already on the car speakerphone, talking to Tony – who was in his car, driving down to Chequers – so Tony could hear our alarm in the background. He offered to ask his driver, Alan, what we should do. I remember noticing an Indian family walking towards us, exquisitely dressed for a wedding.

Feel under the wheel hubs for wires, was Alan's advice. So we both got down on our hands and knees, but I only felt cold slime. 'There's nothing,' says Nick to Tony. 'So what do we do now?'

Tony asked Alan. 'Alan says you'll probably be fine,' says Tony, still on the speaker. 'Yeah sure, of course, you'll be fine. Just try the ignition. Have faith Nick. OK? Speak later,' and he rang off.

So Nick moved his hand towards the ignition and as he did I pulled the children back down the pavement fast, then, seeing the wedding party, now level with the car, I suddenly screamed back: 'Stop! Did he say probably? Don't touch it. Jesus Christ! Stop!'

But I was too late. He'd turned the key.

The wedding family must have thought I was hysterical. Only later – when the bomb squad checked the engine – did they find it had been tampered with. 'We could have been scraping you off the Albert Hall,' they said.

SCENE FIVE

Main diners start coming back into the sitting room, chatting (possibly less important diners leave at this point).

TONY: *(Enters room with C. Goes towards the drinks tray and offers drinks around.)* Armagnac David?

DIRECTOR: So David you get to live in one of these colleges now. A Master – eh! Sounds pretty good to me.

(TOM whispers to NICK.)

DIRECTOR: Whisky. Thanks.

You certainly know how to treat your best men Prime
Minister. There are people in Washington who could take
a few lessons from you. Master... hah. *(NICK whispers to
TONY.)*

TONY: Publish it this week? That leaves us with no time at all.
They can't do that. Can they?

TONY stares up towards NICK.

NICK's phone goes.

NICK: Now? I'll check it out.

Rushes out to the outer office.

DIRECTOR: *(Sitting on a sofa.)* David I've never had the chance
to ask you – where did you cut your teeth in this game?

C: Oh, Budapest in the '70s. Great times.

DIRECTOR: Yeah, remember how agents queued up to sign
on. We knew who the enemy was – not like now. You don't
have to be intelligent to go into intelligence nowadays, as I
was telling... *(Looks around for LAURA who is looking out of the
window.)*

TONY: But err you had some pretty good Iraqi agents too
didn't you David? Like Daisy, the one who turned up
in Germany. He was your best – asset wasn't he. I need
to know more about him, and soon. He's giving a press
conference any time now. Did you know?

C: Prague 1974. You may remember James.

TONY: *(Picking up the ISG report, which is obviously heavy. LAURA
moves closer.)* Look, sorry to talk shop but can we have a
word about this? You've seen the ISG draft. We thought
we'd delayed it getting out there but it now it looks like we
might not be able to hold it back.

C: ISG – bunch of amateurs.

TONY: Yeah, I mean these guys. Look at this. I'm worried what the press are going to make of it…

C: Press? Out there they're not even trying to report the truth Prime Minister.

LAURA: A journalist friend of mine was killed in Baghdad recently. He came from Hebron. Shot dead by American soldiers as he filmed outside Abu Graib for Reuters. The Americans said later they opened fire on him because they thought his camera was a rocket launcher.

C, ignoring her, gets up to pour another drink. TONY continues reading the report.

TOM: *(Coming in.)* Laura, Marisia's on the phone.

LAURA: Marisia?

She rushes out.

SCENE SIX

Outer Office and Stockwell bedroom.

NICK is in the outer office watching the news on the TV and on the phone to MARISIA.

NICK: OK, look, stay calm Marisia and we'll get the police over right away. Here's Laura. *(To LAURA.)* It's OK. She's just panicking about the protesters at the house that's all.

LAURA: That's all! How many are there now? We'll have to get the police there straight away.

Grabs the phone.

As LAURA and MARISIA talk, we see MARISIA in the Stockwell bedroom, sitting hunched up on the floor by the bed. We also hear noise of protesters in the Stockwell street.

NICK: Here's Laura.

LAURA: Marisia what's going on?

MARISIA: Laura they're right outside the door now. Shouting at the house and throwing things.

LAURA: Where are the children?

MARISIA: In the bathroom. They're OK I think. Just frightened. But they have these weapons. Stones I think. Oh my God – I think a brick or something landed on the conservatory.

LAURA: A brick?

(To NICK.) Get the police right away. They're throwing bricks.

NICK: *(To TOM.)* Are the police on their way?

TOM: They're on the way.

MAIRISIA: I'm sitting here near the panic buttons to be safe.

LAURA: Look I'm on my way back OK. Don't worry. OK.

NICK: But you can't leave Laura. There are roadblocks all down Whitehall.

LAURA: Yes. I'll ring back.

I have to get back. You'll have to get the roadblocks moved.

He suddenly turns the volume up. We hear the noise of the helicopters and protesters outside Number Ten on the TV with an echo outside and a slight time lag.

Oh my God.

Paces around ringing her hands.

REPORTER: Downing Street is now virtually under siege here and one protester even managed to gain access to the building. And reports have emerged that the Prime Minister is inside Number Ten tonight holding a secret dinner with intelligence chiefs.

TOM: *(Phone rings, over the top of news report.)* NSC in Washington on the line for you.

REPORTER: Top of the agenda will be the Iraq Survey Group
report which is believed to reveal for the first time that no
weapons of mass destruction have been found in Iraq.

NICK goes up to the screen showing protester on Downing Street terrace.

NICK: *(To TOM.)* Security are on to this I presume.

LAURA: What about security at our house – who's on to that?
Jesus Christ!

NICK: Jack, hi.

LAURA: Marisia.

*NICK trying to sound relaxed, on phone to JACK, the US National
Security Advisor – sense of slight time lag in conversation too.*

NICK: The PM's ready to talk to the President, yes. On the
ISG right? OK. We're hearing that you might ask for
publication to be brought forward.
Well that would put us in a difficult position, Jack. Sure.
No doubt about intention – sure. But can you hold off for
a bit?
Table it? Sorry. What? Oh – *(Laughs.)* – kill it you mean?
No no. Just that table it means the opposite in English. Yes
we all speak the same language. Of course we do.

(Loud laughter, LAURA looks angry.)

OK.

But just one thing Jack are you hearing anything from
Germany? Not good news. On Daisy – they're saying he
was a fraud.
Yes. Sure it's a positive picture overall. On the WMD –
well.

LAURA: Positive – we've got real bricks being thrown…

NICK: Yes, the President's right about that.

LAURA: About what?

NICK: Err. But nothing your end on the German thing then…?

Ok. Thanks. Yes bye Jack.

(To TOM.) How long have we got before the George call?

LAURA: *(To NICK.)* How long have we got before the police get to our house?

TOM: *(To NICK.)* They keep bringing it forward. Now 22.30 GMT.

NICK: So only ten minutes.

(Picks up phone.) Press office…
What. Yeah I'm looking at it.

(Phone rings.)

TOM: Foreign Secretary.

NICK: Hold.

How do they know this? Nobody knows it. Yet. I don't know. Gotta kill it. Pure speculation. Yes.

(To TOM.) Can we page Alastair? We're losing control of this thing and it's not even out there.

I'd better get back.

NICK runs back up to the dining room.

LAURA: There must be some way out of here? Isn't there? Tom? I have to get out.

LAURA follows NICK back to others.

Police are now lining up outside with backs to the windows but nobody inside is aware.

TONY is sitting down again opposite C. LAURA comes in and stands by the window then moves around nervously picking up photographs and watching the others. There is a loud bang outside and she jumps.

C gets out a cigar and TONY offers him a light. NICK stands by waiting.

TONY: *(Answering his phone.)* Hi Janet. Yeah go on. Hold on.

NICK: *(To TONY.)* President is on in ten minutes. And Chirac's holding a press conference as we speak. Going to say he's totally vindicated. I've got a line in to it. Foreign Secretary's been hanging on to speak to you for quite a while. *(Gives TONY a phone.)*

LAURA: Nick.

C, left alone a moment, picks up the ISG report, gets his glasses out and starts looking up the index.

NICK: *(To LAURA.)* I know what you're thinking.

LAURA: I'm thinking I really need to get home. Now. I should never have come.

TONY: *(In the corner of the room.)* Hi Janet. Yes. Yes. Just get the botulism out there… that's it. Doing a terrific job.

(Takes another call.)

C: What news of Chalabi, James?

DIRECTOR: Let's not go there David. *(Pouring drink. To C who puts the report back down.)* You see when I look back it's all so clear David. Rumsfeld sets up his own little CIA over there in the Pentagon. Gets his friends like Chalabi to recruit 'sources' for him, telling the President exactly what he wants to hear, and, we all know, George could never stand up to anyone. Certainly not Rumsfeld. So he doesn't even tell us over at Langley what's going on.

C: So you say.

DIRECTOR: I got no thanks at all – you know that.

TONY comes back to join them.

But here's a man who knows what's what. You pay tribute to those who did their duty Prime Minister as you are doing here tonight. I respect you for that. Really. There've been times when I thought my wife my only loyal supporter in Washington.

TONY: Yeah, where is Abigail tonight? Thought she was coming…

DIRECTOR: *(Turning to Tony.)* To a truly exceptional leader of men. Tony.

TOM appears again, whispers to NICK.

NICK: One minute to the call…

TONY: Well David, time may well be on our side as you say but – err.
Look David what can you give me for George?

C: Buried. In the desert. He got the stuff out to Syria. Can't they see that.

TONY: You're saying it's in Syria now? Is this err up-to-date intelligence? From – from Daisy, for example?

Can I say that to George?

C: It's obvious.

TONY: It's… just… obvious. I see.
So, to be clear David. You're saying it's only a matter of time?

C: Exactly.

TONY: Before we find them.

But I have to have more to say than that. After 18 months these ISG inspectors have found only a handful of botulism seeds. Look page 99. And you see I have no line – at all on Daisy or why we believed him.
There's not even a record.

C pours another drink.

C: History will prove us right.
You put it better than anyone in that dossier Prime Minister.
These suicide bombers can never win.

LAURA: *(Very anxious now, speaking almost to herself but others listen.)* I was at the scene of a suicide bombing once – in Tel Aviv. You don't realise what it is at first but then you notice thousands of tiny pieces of flesh stuck to everything. Plastered over the glass. The broken glass of the shop windows – car bonnets, windscreens, anything. Covered with these little bits.

Sound of another loud crash outside and breaking glass. LAURA jumps back and lets out a slight shriek.

TONY: Don't worry. It's all bomb-proof.

NICK: President's on the line Prime Minister.

TONY and NICK both get up and rush to the Outer Office.

SCENE SEVEN

Outer Office.

TONY: *(To NICK.)* He's half pissed so I can't get anything out of him on Daisy. Its hopeless. Just stalling.

NICK: I can see that. *(Glancing at the TV.)* Maybe you can call in the chips with your friend here.

GEORGE: *(Breathing. Crackling.)* Tony. Yo. Are you there?

TONY: George. Are you there? *(They speak at the same time for a while.)* I'm here.

GEORGE: I'm here.

TONY: I'm here. Here.

GEORGE: Hey, hold on fella. We've got our wires crossed here.

TONY: *(Laughs.)* Well I'm doing fine. Just fine.

GEORGE: Great. Look Tony just a quick one tonight about the ISG.

TONY: It doesn't look too good for us does it?

GEORGE: Well it sure as hell doesn't come up with those WMD. But they're out there. We know that don't we? So don't let it get you down. I'm sure your guys will see it off. Just wanted to let you know that we're just hanging back, playing it down over here.

TONY: Yes, err, but we're told you're planning to publish the report tomorrow, we were wondering if…

GEORGE: Tomorrow? Well I don't know about that but it seems there was some chemical stuff they found somewhere, so we can at least run with that. And you know we're not going to be defeated by this thing.

TONY: Right. No. Of course. But if you could just hold off for a week or so.

GEORGE: Well we're not going to be defeated by this thing you know.

TONY: No, sure. George just one other thing – and sorry to keep you – but are you picking up anything on this strange story out of Germany? There's stuff from Berlin which our guys think is more worrying than the ISG findings. That the source they gave us – you know one that you rated so highly – was some kind of fraudster. They're saying they warned you. Are you picking up on that at all?

GEORGE: What? German sources? Hey since when did the Germans have anything to do with all of this?

TONY: A source they called Daisy. Does that mean anything to you?

GEORGE: Ha Ha Ha. That a joke? Look you're not serious. I know you. Gotta run. You'll handle it great, my friend. You always do. Hey, meant to say, saw your speech the other night. Terrific. Looking good. Whatever happens, your courage will always be remembered.

TONY: *(More nervous laughter.)* Well it might be my epitaph. *(More laughter.)*

GEORGE: Yeah, right. RIP Here lies a man of courage, you mean?

TONY: Right.

Phone goes down.

TONY: This is not looking good Nick. Not good at all. I'm finished if this gets out.

NICK: You are not finished. We can still get ahead of Washington deadlines. Just need a line out.

TONY: I thought you told me you could handle all of this. Do I have to do everything myself.

NICK and TONY run back up.

SCENE EIGHT

Sitting room.

Massive roar from the crowd. This time everyone looks towards the terrace.

TONY: So, David, *(Offering more drinks around.)* where were we? Look we are now out of time on this. *(Pointing at the report.)* Nothing I can do now to stop this getting out there. I've even spoken to the President. So I really do need a line from you on why we believed it. I mean Daisy, was he for real or not?

LAURA and NICK move closer to listen.

The DIRECTOR seems to have nodded off on the sofa.

C: A secondary source handled by the BND. Can't say more than that. You'll understand.
You know I can't discuss the reports of my officers.

TONY: But I am the Prime Minister.

C: With anyone.

TONY: Believe me I don't want to expose any of your guys.

C: You didn't mind exposing Kelly…

TONY: Now hang on a minute…

C: *(Turning to* the *DIRECTOR who is not listening.)* One hundred million the Treasury slashed from our budget last year.

TONY: But the intelligence was drawn from several good sources right? If Daisy blows there were others, right? There's a lot at stake for me here David.

C: Look I told the inquiry all this. We had two prime sources and each passed on material from sub-sources. Though we have since had to discount the two sub-sources as being…

NICK: As being?

C: Unreliable.

TONY: But why didn't you tell me? You didn't tell me. What do you mean unreliable?

LAURA: Yes what do you mean? They weren't telling the truth? What?

TONY and NICK look at her. C looks annoyed.

TOM comes in at this point but NICK signals that he should wait to deliver his message.

TONY: David you didn't tell me any of this before.

C: You didn't ask.

TONY: So where did that leave the prime sources? Let's have it out. Unreliable too. I guess?

NICK: But your guys always interview the prime sources of course – at this level. Surely?

C: In most cases.

TONY: Though not all?

LAURA: So you mean you never saw Daisy? You didn't even see him?

NICK: So who did see him?

TONY: Do you know how we found out about him?

LAURA: Who was he? What was he?

TONY: Yeah, who was he? Do you know anything about him at all?

C: *(Angry. Turning on them.)* Look, this was your war not mine. Your priority Prime Minister – not mine. Our service just did what it was told. You could have read the CX papers just as well as me – the wholesale destruction of Saddam's stockpiles after Desert Storm was on the file for all to see. When you became Prime Minister we didn't tell you he had become a threat again. You told us. We assumed you had your reasons. We trusted in that. And you just asked us to get the proof. 'Don't suck your teeth' – you said. Find evidence and that's exactly what we did. You didn't mind too much what it was, back then.
Oh yes Prime Minister. Oh yes. *(Reeling slightly.)*
And you and I will be proved right yet. Of that I'm sure. Surer than I've ever been. *(Reeling and reaching for another drink.)*

TONY: David, I understand that of course but...

C: I gave you information that no other service could provide and you were grateful. GCHQ were out of the game. The Americans had nobody out there. *(Looks at the DIRECTOR who has nodded off.)* So I gave you the very best we had on the ground. Without us you'd have had no case at all. *(Picking up the report and slamming it shut.)* No – it's no good laying this at my door now.
It wasn't me who wrote that dossier.
No... you didn't want the ifs and buts – or so you said. Go out there and find the stuff you said. Let's not waste our time, let's get it done. No reason that it can't be done.
So why all the questions now?

TONY: Look David, you know, I understand all that, believe me, but – what I need to know right now is why the hell did we believe in Daisy?

The DIRECTOR suddenly hears this and wakes up, standing up and butting in loudly.

DIRECTOR: Oh Daisy! I can help you all with that. And let me say here and now – as we are, indeed, among friends – that I am not to blame for that one. No Sir! That Daisy idea was all cooked up by Rumsfeld in the Oval Office. I had nothing to do with those sources of his. Don't know where they conjured them up from. Rumsfeld just presented what they said to the President.

And then I said the Brits will never fall for it. Rumsfeld could be a real asshole you know, excuse my language. Here's the thing Prime Minister – we weren't sure you wanted to join our war. And we in the CIA understood that. But all Rumsfeld understood was that he needed your base at Diego Garcia so badly he was prepared to feed you a barefaced lie.

That's the way this administration is, you see. That's what I was trying to explain to you. They don't do duty, loyalty. That stuff… No, not my style at all.

C scoffs, gets up and walks over to the window.

Rumsfeld!

LAURA watches all four carefully.

NICK: So Daisy was a sham. That's our answer is it? *(Looks round at TONY.)*

How do you suggest we 'handle' this one?

TONY pours himself a drink.

DIRECTOR: I thought you people would see through it in no time. Daisy! You didn't really believe it did you? I mean, Prime Minister, I thought I'd signalled that pretty strongly when we all met at the Azores.

TONY: Azores? *(Looks at NICK and at C.)*

The DIRECTOR looks hard at TONY, who looks around the room and sees everyone now looking at him. Roar from protesters. He is speechless. Staring ahead. NICK gets up, throws the report down on the table as TOM enters and starts to speak.

C: I have to go. Last train to Cambridge.

LAURA: Can we all go then? I have to go too.

TOM: It's impossible for anyone to leave. Latest is there's been a bomb scare in Trafalgar Square.

TOM leaves for Outer Office followed by NICK and LAURA.

LAURA rushes out.

Louder shouting from the crowd.

SCENE NINE

Number Ten Outer Office.

NICK rushes into Outer Office followed by LAURA and TOM.

Phones ringing. TOM picks them up.

LAURA: Nick.

NICK: What? Please… can't you see…

LAURA: But.

TOM: Nick I have Alastair on conference line one.
And the Elysee on two.
Bill Barker of North West trains on three. Six dead in a crash near Sedgefield.

NICK switches news to pictures of a train accident.

And Marisia again on line four for you Laura.

LAURA: *(Picks up phone quickly.)* Marisia? Oh thank God for that. Good. All of them? Well hold tight and I'll be back as soon as I can. Yes. Well done Marisia. You're wonderful. Thanks.

NICK: Bill.

Puts phone down.

LAURA: Police have arrived. Protesters have gone.

NICK: Good. Tom – get me Barker back – no hang on.
Put Alastair on the speaker phone could you and get the
Prime Minister down.

ALASTAIR: Hello

NICK: Hold on Alastair.

TOM: And Gerry Adams is calling back in 20 minutes. The on-
the-runs can't wait, he says.

ALASTAIR: I've come out of the match, so this'd better be
good.

NICK: Sorry, look, I've had protesters outside our house
scaring the children and…

ALASTAIR: I'm not here to sort out your domestic
arrangements…

TONY now joins the others in the Outer Office.

NICK: Look the Americans are going to publish the ISG report
tomorrow. No warning.

ALASTAIR: What? Tomorrow? I leave you guys alone for five
minutes…

TONY: *(To TOM)* Get me the Chief Whip.

NICK: *(To ALASTAIR)* Hang on. You're the one who got your
wires crossed with Washington this time – you said you'd
bought us two weeks.

LAURA: Aren't you going to tell him? About Daisy? Are you
going to tell anyone? Is anyone going to tell anyone?

TOM: Chief Whip's holding on line four.

NICK: Just give me the top line for the press on the ISG OK
and I'll put it out tonight. *(Looks at watch.)* Can still meet
Washington deadlines. Get ahead of the game here. It's

PMQs tomorrow. *(Looking at TONY who is picking up phone to Chief Whip.)*

TONY: Yeah, can you get over here in *(Looks at clock.)* half an hour?

ALASTAIR: OK just stick to 'This is NOT OUR report' – OK. Not ours. So we can keep some distance from it at all times. Throw as much as you can back at the Americans. Just remember, deployment of defensive lines.

TONY: If the final report says what we think then I might have to resign and that'll be your line Alastair.

ALASTAIR: Come off it. Over this?

TONY starts to leave room but halts as LAURA says:

LAURA: No. Not over this. Over Daisy.

ALASTAIR: What? Come on what the fuck happened over Daisy. Laura... *(Menacing.)*

NICK: It's not great.

NICK and TONY look at LAURA.

LAURA: It was all a hoax. Rumsfeld hoaxed you not Saddam.

ALASTAIR: Oh so that's what they're saying now is it? Hah, Is that what our American friend told you tonight – if you believe that you'll believe anything.

TONY: Really Laura you know. I mean whatever may have been said upstairs...

NICK: May have been. May? *(Turns and looks at TONY. Angry.)* Why may have been said? I think we all heard him pretty clearly this time didn't we? We've been well and truly shafted. You're going to have to sit down and think very carefully about what this means – for all of us.

TONY: *(Looks at both of them. Pauses.)* Get a grip Nick. What's got into you?

You know as well as I do that James is a bitter man. And he was knocking it back up there like there was no tomorrow.

NICK: Oh for God's sake. You have to face up to this. I'll speak to the JIC and see if I can...

TONY: Look, what? Why the? It's... just between us isn't it. They knew that?

NICK walks off, stares out of the window. Sits. Head in hands. Exasperated.

ALASTAIR: *(On loudspeaker still.)* Hello? Hello? Anyone there? Hellooo. OK I'm out of here. *(Rings off.)*

NICK: We'll just have to find a way of – I don't know. I'll do my best, but I really don't know...

TONY: Right.

LAURA: *(Narrating, thinking aloud.)* You're all going to do nothing then. Is that it?

TOM: Prime Minister we have authority for the guests to leave by the side entrance. We're bringing them down. I've arranged outriders for C and the Director.

TONY: I'd better get back to the guests. *(Leaves.)*

Long pause as LAURA and NICK are left alone, watching each other, unsure what to do or say. TOM is on the phone.

LAURA: We can't carry on pretending now Nick.

NICK: So what do you suggest? I mean we can hardly go out to the microphones out there in the front of Number Ten and announce that the Prime Minister was hoaxed into war by Donald Rumsfeld. Can we?

LAURA: Why not? It's true.
You said it Nick. Shafted. Your word again – not mine.

Pause.

Well if nobody else is going to do it. I will.

NICK: What?

LAURA: Tell them.

NICK: You?

LAURA: Yes. Yes. If no one else will. I will – I have to.

NICK: You?

LAURA: Yes me. It's very clear. It's what I have to do.

NICK: How? Who to?

LAURA: Like you said. I have to go out to those reporters on the doorstep and tell them what has happened.

NICK: Walk out under the lights to those microphones and make a statement. Are you mad? The consequences would be catastrophic.

LAURA: Consequences?

NICK: Just think what'll happen.

LAURA: Watch me. I'll go now. *(Gets up.)*

TOM: *(Who had been listening carefully.)* They won't let you out.

LAURA: They have to eventually.

NICK: And we'll… they'll all deny it – here. Have you not learned anything?

Words of a bitter man – that's how they'll kill it. You heard the line from Tony already. Alastair's probably already being briefed ahead of Daisy's press conference. Washington'll just deny.
They'll shoot it down, kill it dead.

LAURA: You mean nobody will believe me?

NICK: Course not. You can't just – tell the truth like that. Nobody can.
Where's the proof?
There is not a single record about Daisy, you know. Not a trace in any of the Iraq papers.
He asked me to run a check earlier today and there's

nothing on it. Files are clean. Not a word in the JIC reports, nothing in the CX papers, and no mention in Butler or Hutton. Nothing anywhere. I looked through everything. All those emails – you saw, remember? I read them all again and more. Trying to work out how we got from where we were to – where we are. There's going to be another inquiry you see…

LAURA: I have my note.
　　The one I leant you this morning. Where is it? You do still have it don't you Nick?

He waits a moment. Then pulls it out.

NICK: This?

LAURA: I'll have it back now please.

NICK: *(Reads it.)* Sonofabitch, ready to offload. Jesus. Hah!

LAURA: *(Tries to take it back.)* I want it back. It's mine.
　　And it's very precious now. *(Turning it over.)*
　　What's this bit?
　　Nick – doesn't trust German source.
　　Tells Tony they're 'clutching at straws'.

NICK: Did I say that? We were so boxed in, you see. And Daisy was just one of hundreds of things that were thrown at us. You should have seen the piles of paper in the Cabinet Office today. A mountain of it. I tried to follow the trail this time – I really did. To retrace our steps from A to B. But I couldn't figure out how we got to…

LAURA: What?

They both turn, stunned, watching TONY, C and the DIRECTOR walk through towards the side exit.

NICK: Where we didn't want to be. *(Turns back to her.)* So many false summits you see.

LAURA: You started from the wrong place.

NICK: And then we couldn't get back.

We now see TONY shaking hands with departing guests and saying goodbye.

LAURA and NICK stand watching. TOM also watches from his seat.

DIRECTOR: Prime Minister, a memorable evening. Truly. So generous of you to host it.

TONY: *(To the DIRECTOR and C.)* Really good to see you both and, well, you know, I firmly believe that.

C: History will prove us right. *(Slurring his words.)* No doubt about that. Those weapons are out there.

TONY: Yeah, well as you know I'm certainly with you on that… yeah… And look, David err we'll… we'd better touch base on all of this… Tomorrow. Agree some words on it. OK? Yeah. Bye.

Just before C exits he stops, turns and looks at LAURA.

C: From *The Independent* I hear.

Makes a sign of a cross with two forefingers and holds it up at her.

LAURA: *(Roar of protesters. She looks out of the window.)* There is another way you know. I suddenly see it. I do. I really do. So simple.

NICK: What?

LAURA: You have to come out there with me.
That's it. It's so obvious. You have to walk out of the front door with me and face the cameras. Back me up. We both heard it. We both know it's true. We both tell them what we've heard.

NICK: Me. Now you have gone mad.

LAURA: No it's the only way. Everyone trusts you, you see. Everyone would believe you. You have to do it Nick. You've done enough for him. You really have. Do this for me.

LAURA goes over to NICK's desk and holds out a hand.

He sits down again. Strangely calm. Looks at her. Swivels on chair again. Round and round. Turns up the TV which is showing the protesters outside again. During this conversation the two seem oblivious to things around them.

NICK: So what you're saying is we should both walk out there and announce what's happened here tonight. Hold a kind of press conference?
Well, that is one way, I grant you that. *(Chuckles to himself. Quoting something.)* 'We go together – I with you and you with me'.

LAURA: Come on.

TONY now walks back across the room having finally seen off the DIRECTOR out of the side door. LAURA watches him walk past and seems to be going to say something to him but she turns to the audience instead.

(Narrating.) And I was about to ask him if he'd really believed in Daisy – when he looked upwards to the light and said…

TONY: But would it have been better to have done nothing at all?

(Turns to her.) You'll play straight with me tonight Laura won't you?

LAURA: *(Narrating.)* So I said nothing – turning his words over in my head 'you'll play straight with me' and thinking what a peculiar sort of world they'd come from and then…

NICK turns up the TV volume suddenly. They all look up at the TV which shows a grainy picture of C. Then a picture of TONY. The words 'breaking news' flash across the screen. NICK now turns up the volume so it is quite loud.

NEWS READER: Calls for the resignation of the Prime Minster are mounting tonight following dramatic revelations that vital evidence on Iraq's weapons of mass destruction was a hoax. Reliable sources have told Sky News that the US concocted fake evidence about the threat from Saddam in order to persuade the Prime Minster to back the war.

According to a Downing Street insider, the Prime Minster was told tonight for the first time that the intelligence was faked during a meeting with intelligence chiefs in Downing Street. The Leader of the Opposition, says if the revelations are true the Prime Minister should resign. He says Britain was hoaxed by its closest ally into joining the Iraq war.

As this report is underway TONY moves closer to the TV and stares at it. NICK and LAURA stand behind him. Phones go.

NICK: Tom get on to the press office. Get Alastair.

TONY: How the hell did this get out there? Where's Tom?

LAURA: He's gone.

LAURA walks over to TOM's desk. Sees he's taken everything.

He's taken the photo of his dad. It was Tom who told them.

NICK and TONY now look at TOM's empty desk. Then at LAURA. Then back at the TV. Then a phone starts to ring. Then another and another. Both NICK's mobiles ring. LAURA's phone also rings. Nobody answers them.

After a few moments LAURA picks up her bag and coat to leave then comes back and picks up photographs from NICK's desk. Then she leaves.

SCENE TEN

Lights now go down on TONY and NICK as they remain standing staring at the TV screen.

LAURA then re-enters and stands apart from them at the front of the stage.

LAURA: *(Narrating.)* I went straight home after that. I could hardly get near the house at first. The police cordon went all around, but there were no protesters left. Inside the children and Marisia were all asleep.

They'd broken a window in the new conservatory. But that was the only damage.

I knew Nick wouldn't be back for hours and I stayed up all night watching the TV in bed as the Daisy story broke relentlessly in ever-bigger waves of revelation and condemnation. Statements were rushed out in London and Washington and in the small hours – our time – George spoke on the White House lawn, denying any knowledge of it all and throwing it all back on to the CIA. As dawn broke the story was so confused that few could understand where it had begun. Nick called me a few times to ask how I thought it was playing. By mid-morning Tony was planning his press conference.

Then Daisy beat him to it. Appeared before the press in Berlin. Live.

I couldn't believe it. There he was. The man who took us to war. Jeans, T-shirt, unshaven. Spoke no English. A scruffy looking lawyer next to him. Turned out Daisy was an Iraqi truck driver. He'd gone to Germany and offered some nonsense on WMD and fed it to the German authorities in return for getting status as a refugee. Said he'd once had a friend with a brother who worked in one of Saddam's secret military facilities for a week or so. But they'd never even met. He didn't remember any British interrogators. But he didn't remember much. Said he'd tried to retract but nobody would listen to him. He was sorry for all the trouble.

The next day of course all hell broke loose and everyone seemed to be calling for his resignation.

At midday came the announcement that the Prime Minister would hold a press conference within the hour. He walked out alone to the microphones looking around a little wild-eyed. Almost exhilarated. But determined. Made a statement. Took only a handful of questions. Said intelligence chiefs would have to answer for the confusion. But he'd always done what he believed was right.

NICK comes over and stands behind her.

Then it was all over.

NICK: We always knew he'd go one day.

LAURA: No more calls. Cut off for good.

NICK: I'm looking forward to the Dolomites.

LAURA: I'll always regret not asking him if he really believed in Daisy.

NICK: Look… *(Slightly annoyed.)* Whatever else… he did believe all that. *(Now talking to the audience.)* He believed it. Believe me. *(LAURA looks at him. Seems to be resisting an argument.)*

LAURA: Did he ever suspect me of leaking it I wonder?

NICK: *(Shrugs.)* I don't think he gave that a lot of thought.
Tom's confession note came the next day.
He also named his successor – did I tell you that.
(Chuckles.)
It's a tradition of the Duty Clerk to do that.

Pause.

I wonder if you'd really have done it though – walked out and told the press. If Tom hadn't got there first.

LAURA: Of course. I was all ready.
And you'd have come with me wouldn't you? You'd have backed me up. You couldn't have stuck with him? Could you? Surely? Not after that.

LAURA moves away from NICK a little and looks hard at him, as if she's not quite sure.

Ends.